Forty Days

by
Steven M. Cannon

"For Cancer Fighters, Dreamers and Believers Everywhere"

"For Cancer Fighters, Dreamers, and Believers Everywhere"

Forward

Steve Cannon runs. He does not actually call himself a runner though, and thinks of himself more as an adventurer. He has completed the Tuscobia Winter 150 twice on his fat bike, and has biked the Actif Epica and the 2016 Arrowhead 135. In 2016, he was inducted into The Order of the Hrimthurs. He has run nearly a hundred marathons, has tamed 36-hour adventure races, has failed and nearly died on the Yukon River Quest and finished the Equalizer 24-hour endurance run. In 2004, he rode his bike to the start line of the Deadwood Mickleson Trail Marathon in South Dakota...from Iowa. He has completed 18 RAGBRAIs and five Ride the Rockies, and has ridden the gravel three times in the Dirty Kanza 200. In 2009 he ran across his home state of Iowa (292 miles in 11 days) and was the first person ever to run around the great Lake Michigan (1037 miles in 40 days), averaging a marathon's distance a day. His adventures have raised money for Livestrong, Camp Kesem and Above and Beyond Cancer. His run around Lake Michigan in 2012 was covered by Iowa Public Radio, the Huffington Post, and NBC Sports, and is the subject of this book, Forty Days.

Steve's adventures have led him to unique insights into setting goals, dreaming big dreams, challenging oneself, and uncovering the universal laws which apply to success in all things. He shares these insights through his speaking, coaching, and online courses. You can learn more at www.expandyourpossible.com.

Day 1

Set your goal, identify the first step needed and take it.

Years of running led me to this place. *How had this become my life? Would I have what it took to make this run? Had my appetite for adventure set me up for an epic fail?* I never ran in high school or college. I hated running. Many years ago, I ran a 5k just to meet girls after moving to Colorado. *Now this? What the hell was I thinking?!?!*

I sat alone at the end of the bed in the Chicago Hilton contemplating those questions. The alarm would not blast for a few more hours; I had set it the night before, knowing I would not need it. It was May 27th, at 4:30 in the morning. In just five hours I would begin my attempt to become the first person to run around Lake Michigan. The journey would cover over a thousand miles and be equal to running a marathon a day for forty straight days.

I wished that I could sleep those few remaining hours, but my brain was in overdrive. Every effort at meditation was quickly interrupted. *What am I doing? Am I crazy? What if I fail? It's so hot! I*

FORTY DAYS

might not be able to do this with two healthy feet, let alone two injured ones. Months of training had resulted in a nagging case of plantar fasciitis, an inflammation of the ligaments running from the heel to the arch of the foot.

As one doubt would leave me, two more would take its place. I took a few deep breaths and asked for the strength to make it through Day One. If this venture was going to succeed, staying in the moment would be crucial, one day, one hour, one step at a time. *We can all take one step,* I reminded myself.

To keep taking those steps, I would need to eat. Eight thousand calories was the number my team and I had reached through testing and months of training. We determined that I'd burn about 700 calories an hour running at a pace of ten to twelve minutes per mile. This would not be a race, far from it. A race would demand a much faster pace and burn many more calories. A faster pace would also put far more stress on my body. The only goal was to reach Day Two in as close to the same shape as I had been on Day One. This would require two things: patience and *calories*. To disregard either of these would eventually result in failure. Run too fast, and the body would break down physically. Consume too few calories, and the body would not recover in time to allow another day of twenty-six miles.

Three years earlier, while running across my home state of Iowa, I had learned this lesson well. It was the eighth day of an eleven-day marathon journey to raise money for the Livestrong Foundation. The temperatures had been challenging. Highs near 100 degrees and equally nasty humidity made the going tough. Eating was a real issue in those conditions. My body temperature soared, and the first casualty was my appetite. I didn't feel like eating, so I didn't. Not getting enough calories was like firing a gun where the bullet didn't hit until a few days later. I was in big trouble; I just didn't know it.

I had just passed the 200 mile mark and had stopped to celebrate with what I hoped would be a few cheeseburgers. Once in the cafe, it took time for me to be able to eat, but slowly it became possible. By all accounts I should have been starving, and I loved cheeseburgers back then. One burger, some fries, and a Pepsi were all I could handle. When we left the cafe, I started feeling super tired. I didn't want to ask the support crew to stop, but I was suddenly trashed. The bullet was in the air and closing in on me. I laid down in the RV for an hour-long nap. When I woke up, I didn't feel much better, but I was used to that. I got up and started moving again.

A mile or so down the road, a sharp pain shot out from just above my knee on the lower outside portion of my thigh. There's a saying in ultra-running, "If something hurts, don't pay too much attention to it. Something else will take its place soon enough." It was a good rule and surprisingly true. The point of the saying is to accept occasional discomfort, as it will pass. So I did just that. This time, however, it did not pass. The pain was odd; it was moving very slowly, like a worm looking for a place to call home. I tried to ignore it as I had so many other "discomforts," but this was different. The sensation had moved nearly halfway up my outer thigh when it found its home. The bullet had just hit me. The pain stopped me in my tracks. The past few days of not getting enough food into the tank had left my body no option but to shut down. I would spend the rest of that day's seven miles and the entire twenty-eight miles the next day forced to walk. That was only an eleven-day run. This

FORTY DAYS

would be forty potentially hotter days.

Navy Pier in Chicago was to be the launch site for the run, Harry Caray's Tavern to be exact. Harry Caray had been a sportscaster whose career had culminated in a decade and a half stint as the popular announcer for the Chicago Cubs, and I have been a life-long Chicago Cubs fan. My dedication to the Cubs was linked with memories of my Grandma Rachel and Grandpa Bill, who had been a very special part of my life. I was lucky to be able to spend a lot of time with them while they were alive. I can still remember Grandma going to bed on those summer nights listening to the Cubbies and Harry Caray on her bedside radio. She died years ago from lung cancer. I wanted to run for her and for everyone dealing with this terrible disease. She would have thought it was pretty cool starting at Harry Caray's.

I met Brian at the hotel cafe for breakfast. He was fired up, which was no surprise. He would be blogging everyday, keeping everyone up to date with all that was happening. Brian was an old college roommate, and he had become an accomplished writer over the past several years. He had plenty of questions. Most fell short, un-able to penetrate the fog. I was a bundle of nerves. My mind was scrambling. This way, then that. I couldn't eat. I stuffed a few bites down but was almost nauseous. The run was scheduled to start at 9 a.m. We left the Hilton around 8 a.m. and headed for Navy Pier.

We stepped outside, and the RV was there ready to go. Jarred had obviously been up early. I hadn't spent one moment the previous evening or that morning worrying about the RV or Jarred. That was the one thing I knew would not be an issue with this run. Jarred was not only a dear friend, he was also the mother of all sup-

6

port people—a true renaissance man. He could fix anything, could cook like your granny, and had a heart of gold. He was the ultimate safety blanket, and he would be with me the whole way.

It was necessary to start at nine instead of earlier; friends and family, some of whom had traveled quite a way, would run with me that day. It hadn't seem right asking them to start at six in the morning. Had it been just me, that would have been the target; temperatures were already soaring.

We all gathered in front of Harry Caray's. It was a great atmosphere. Everyone was psyched to be a part of the send-off, and it was really moving that these people were there to support me and the run. The time to go was nearly upon us. The RV sat on the road in front of Harry's, the back of it covered with sponsors' logos and a few handwritten notes of encouragement from folks back home; it would be our support vehicle for the entire journey. We all assembled in front of the logos, and I said a few words of thanks and about why we were there.

We all shared a common bond. Cancer had touched all of our lives in one way or another. I'm sure, as we all stood there, everyone thought about those they love. Some had won the fight, and some had lost it. *I believe that each time we remember someone who has died, that it brings them back to us. They are summoned to share with us again all that we had loved about them.* There were hundreds of remembered souls who ran with us as we left that morning. It was a moment that will always stay with me.

It felt so good to be underway—a huge relief actually. The incessant chattering of my mind the past few days had become nearly unbearable. Now the game was on. Everyone's spirits were sky high. I can only guess that they too were running with thoughts of loved ones in the cancer fight, and certainly their contributions to the run honored those loved ones.

Our crew had a few people on bikes and a half dozen others who would run with me for a while. Maria and Jeff Davis had brought their kids with them from Des Moines. It was cool to have the kids along; their youthful energy and belief in all things was contagious. "Black Jack" Noble, his wife Laura, and their kids were there as well. Jack had always been a running inspiration to me. He had been marathoning and knocking down 50k and fifty-milers long before it was cool. Had he not been getting ready for his first hundred-miler in a few weeks, he would have probably stayed with me a few days.

One of the unseen benefits of this run was that it had brought many old friends back into contact. It had been years since I had seen my old roommate Trent and his wife. Trent and his family had also made the drive over to Chicago from Des Moines to see me off.

Our send-off group also included hometown flavor; Kristan, my sister and best friend, along with her husband, Michael, were there from their home in Aurora, Illinois. We also had a nice crew of friends from there in Chicago. Ryan Nestor, an incredibly talented architect and lifelong Cubs fan, had been a huge help setting everything up with Harry Caray's for the send-off. Harry Caray's was one of his clients, and the restaurant was a great host.

Lake Michigan was a beautiful dark shade of blue, and her size incomprehensible. I had the utmost respect for her. There is a saying in mountain climbing that you don't climb the mountain; the mountain allows you to climb it. The idea being, you better respect her, because if she decides to spit you off, there is nothing you can do about it. Nothing. The night prior I had asked the great lake for her blessing. If I was going to make it around this lake, I would need her help.

As the miles clicked by, and the temperature clicked higher, people slowly began to fade away. Every few miles someone would need to turn around. We shared a special hug each time. I couldn't adequately put into words how grateful I was for their support. I hope they felt it in my hugs.

At the thirteen mile point, the running crew was now my brother-in-law Michael and I. The bike trail along the lake had run out, and we were in the concrete jungle. The weatherman's ominous forecast was spot on; it was well on its way to the hottest May 27th *ever* in Chicago. Lake Michigan was about a half mile away, and without her breeze it was stifling. Michael had recently completed a marathon and was hanging tough. We were doing our best to joke about how damn hot it was, but we were both suffering.

We came upon a sign, not long after passing Northwestern University, that let us know a beach lay just a few blocks to our right. The support vehicle was a couple miles straight ahead. Heading for the beach ensured us a respite from the heat, but we were not sure how we would proceed once we got there. We decided to go for it. That choice would seal Michael's fate for the rest of the day and nearly bring me to my knees.

The lake looked so inviting. A slightly refreshing breeze blew off her, and we headed down to get our hands and hats into the lake for a quick cooling. We used our hats like ladles, scooping up as much water as they would hold and dumping them onto our heads. It felt *so* good. We had been cooking, and this relief made it seem as if we had made a wise choice. It was my hope we could

FORTY DAYS

run close to the water for a couple miles in the hard-packed sand and then head back out on the road to find Jarred and the RV. Unfortunately, the sand was not packed nearly hard enough, and the waves of the lake pushed us back into the softer sand every few steps. The sun had heated that sand to the point that it was almost unbearable. You either ran close to the water on a bit of a slope dancing back and forth or you stayed on the flat sinking into the soft sand with each step.

Michael and I were no longer trying to make light of our choice. This was tough sledding, and it was each man for himself. We needed to get off this beach as fast as possible. It was another mile or so to the end. Once there we could climb the stairs and get back to the streets. Looking back, it was the toughest one mile of the run.

The stairs leaving the beach were no treat, but they were solid. The RV was waiting not far away. Safely out of the Sahara, we laughed about how much that sucked, and we soaked up as much fluids and air-conditioning as we could. Michael let me know he was probably done but would hang on until the end of the next stretch and see how he was feeling. He had been a warrior. The fifteen or so miles he put in that day were as hard as any marathon I had ever done. Hard as hell. I was so grateful for his tenacity and companionship. The training wheels were off now. There would be no one to chat away the miles. It was 103 degrees, and I still had eleven or twelve miles to go, solo.

My sister Kristan and their daughter Alyssa met us to pick Michael up. We shared stories from the day and hugs as they left Jarred, Tobin, and me to our task. Tobin had been a great help so far. He kept us company on his bike, supplying much needed fluids. He had become a good friend over the past few years and would be staying these first few days with us. The run suddenly felt very real. Butterflies were long gone, burnt off by the miles and heat. I jogged away from the RV and watched my family drive off out of the neighborhood we had stopped in, headed back home to Aurora. It was time to get down to business. If this run was going to happen, it would be necessary to get into the moment and stay there. That work was now beginning; it was just me and the voices in my head. Without anyone to chat with, I suddenly realized how noisy it was up there. The voices would get louder before they would get quieter and hopefully go away completely.

The goal of the run was simple. Circle the world's sixth largest lake and raise as much money as possible for the twenty-eight million people dealing with cancer worldwide. On a personal level, it would be the deepest inner journey I had ever undertaken. It would become a forty-day meditation, a stripping off of all the BS that doesn't really matter in our lives. I wanted to find the best of me, and to do that I'd also have to deal with the worst of me.

Tobin was a great addition to the team. We did not know each other well before the run, though our paths had crossed from time to time at different races or social functions. The time spent leading up to this run had brought us closer. I had found out that he had reasons beyond just his desire for adventure to join us. He had recently lost his mother to cancer, and I believe the run helped him reconcile that and feel closer to her. He is a great photographer, and the images he posted those first few days really captured the essence of our journey. Friends and family ate 'em up. I think it made them feel as if they were a little bit closer to us. It was a real blessing having him there.

As we took a short break in a city park, Tobin mentioned a

limestone trail may be waiting for us soon. Damn, it was hot. As the three of us sat in the park sweating all over the place, a sense of adventure was palpable. It was just us. We had come over 20 miles. Hopefully, Tobin's forecast of softer trail was correct. It was only Day One, but running on hard surfaces was something to be avoided whenever possible. Each step had value. Each step required respect. Stay in the moment.

Tobin's map skills proved correct, and a half mile out of the park we were on a beautiful tree-lined, crushed limestone path. The music was blasting in my ears as we began running into the small town of Highland Park. Twenty-six miles were in the tank, and in just a mile and a half we would meet Jarred at a strip mall parking lot that would be home for the evening.

I felt a surge of energy. It was Memorial Day, and people were out on the patios enjoying drinks and food. Running past them, I felt like my old buddy Forrest Gump cruising by. I was on a great running adventure and living my dream. Adrenaline was a great thing. We had left Navy Pier twenty-seven miles behind us. My legs felt the best they had all day. Heat and distance be damned. Jarred, Tobin, and I shared high fives and giant hugs. Day One was in the bag.

The key to multi-day runs lay not so much in the day-to-day running but rather in the upkeep of your body, starting each day as close to the same place physically as the day before. It was a simple goal but not an easy one. The day's heat had made eating solid food nearly impossible, and Jarred had been letting me know all day that we were *way* behind. Thanks to Hammer Nutrition and a good bit of chocolate milk, I had about 4000 calories of my 8000 calorie daily goal in me. The fitness app we were using told us at that rate

I'd finish the run about 50 pounds lighter. It apparently did not have an "eat more or you are screwed" setting. The real truth was that I wouldn't be able to finish the run on only 4000 calories per day.

As soon as I got in the RV, I immediately slammed a couple recovery drinks and headed for a cold shower. Although late in the day, the temperature was still near 100 degrees, and if I was going to be able to throw the feed bag on, my body temperature needed to come down. The cold shower was shocking! It had been a long day in the heat, but once the initial burst of cold water hit me, I slowly got used to it.

Jarred has many skills. High on this list is that the dude can cook! He went straight to work preparing dinner. He was a modern-day chuckwagon man, with a portable cooking setup that was serious business. By the time I wrestled my recovery tights on, stretched and got outside, chow was ready.

The cold shower woke up the beast inside me, and it was hungry. I ate, ate, and ate some more. I doubt the quality of food would have mattered, but it was delicious. Jarred had thrown together a chicken pasta worthy of any Italian restaurant. Spirits were high as we all sat next to the RV in the empty lot and reveled in the energy.

Darkness began to fall, and it was time for bed. I didn't really want to leave Tobin and Jarred. It would have been great to sit around and tell stories all evening. After running and eating, part three was just as important: rest. The RV was nice and cool, thanks to the generator powering the AC. Even after the shower, my body was still hot. The AC would make sleep bearable. Without it, sleep would be impossible. I lay down and contemplated the day. I passed out almost immediately. I'd like to think with a big smile on

FORTY DAYS

my face. Day Two would be upon us soon. Too soon.

I woke up in a pile of sweat and a haze. *What time was it? Why was I so hot?!?! What the hell happened to the air conditioning?*

I stumbled out of bed. Outside, I found Jarred fiddling with the generator. *What the hell,* I thought, *we just bought this thing.* Another of Jarred's many skill is that he can fix anything. It was about 1:00 a.m. The clock was ticking. This thing needed to be fixed and fixed fast. Sleeping or not sleeping depended on it.

We tried everything. The damn thing just would not fire. I held my tongue, as it was well past two in the morning now, and this was serious business. Jarred and Tobin were doing everything they could, and voicing my frustration wasn't going to make anything better. The thought of attacking Day Two on a couple hours of sleep weighed heavily on me. "Is there anything you can do about it?" I asked myself. The answer was "no." Accept it and move on. Acceptance would be one of the most important tools at my disposal over the next thirty-nine days. I crawled back into bed and sweated out a few more hours of sleep: not the start to Day Two I was hoping for.

Day 2

See it. Accept it. Deal with it. Next.

Scott Jurek, a world class distance runner, writes about acceptance in his book *Eat and Run.* He gives a very cool checklist of the mental questions he goes through when things get tough. The book is a great read and is about so much more than running.

Acceptance. Was there anything I could do about the generator taking a crap? Nope. Emotional energy was a valuable commodity. Bitching and moaning about something that couldn't be fixed was a waste of that energy. *Acceptance.* I had been able to get a few hours sleep, rolling around in my own sweat. I was dealing with an overnight low temperature of 80-plus degrees and a body that was still kicking off its own heat after cooking in Mother Nature's oven that first day.

Life is always about perspective. Two people given the exact same scenario can absorb it and process it in two completely opposing ways. *Perspective.* How I choose to process life's challenges will determine not only the outcome of those situations but also, in broader terms, the quality of the life I will lead.

People fighting cancer learn this lesson better than most. I was dealing with a hot night's sleep. *Perspective.* Anyone heading into chemotherapy that day, or any other day, would gladly trade places with me. Those people are heroes. They have taught me what is really important in life, and what is not; what is a real struggle, and what is not. I do my best to honor and give thanks for the gifts I have been given every day.

Before long, it was 7:30 a.m. I was fed, it was a beautiful sunny day, and I got to go running. Acceptance and perspective. Those battling cancer have taught me the real meaning of those two words. This run would be my *thank you.*

Human beings are made for adventure. We are made to seek out and explore new places: to run, to bike, to hike, to play! It is inherent in us all. I believe it is what makes up our souls. We were not made to live nine-to-five sitting in a cube. We were not made to sit in traffic jams to and from work. Life is a gift, and it is to be lived to the fullest. *Now!*

When we adventure, our souls scream with pleasure. Everything is better. We feel better about ourselves. Our relationships are better. Work is better. We smile more; we bitch less. We can easily get into a rut stacking forty, fifty, even sixty-hour weeks one atop another, but that is not living. Continue down that path long enough, and the soul will suffocate. I have never understood the idea of working hard while you are young, so that when you are old and unable to move, you can retire and watch the grass grow or the paint dry. It does not have to be one or the other. You can have it all.

It was Day Two. The sun was shining, and after only just a few minutes of walking that scream of pleasure hit me. A giant smile crossed my face. I was on an adventure. My future was uncertain. What lay ahead of me, there was no way to know. What I did know was that eventually the day would end, and there would be great stories from this day. Twenty-six miles to go. My soul was happy.

The excitement of finally being on the run filled me with energy. I loved the intensity of all the training, but scaling back and tapering these past few weeks had been maddening. "Tapering" is the process of letting the body heal and grow stronger in the weeks prior to an event. It is also a bit like caging a wild animal. Sure it was only Day Two, but we were officially in it. I would also be crossing into a new state today: Wisconsin. That seemed pretty cool. The Michigan state line would not come nearly as quick. I was slowly clipping off the miles, while Jarred was working behind the scenes to make sure we slept more comfortably our next thirty-nine nights. Which is to say, he was working on getting the generator fixed. The temperature was rising fast, and the forecast said at or near 100 degrees would be the deal again today. I had no doubts Jarred would figure it out. He always figured it out.

We came upon a state park somewhere around the thirteen-mile mark. My pace had been pretty slow, which I was okay with. Patience would be key on this run. This was not a race, and nothing good would come from pushing too fast in these temperatures. By this time it was *hot*, and because of that I had eaten very little. The park had a nice beach—time to take a dip.

We parked the RV and headed for the water. The beach was busy. This being a holiday weekend, people were everywhere. Lake Michigan's blue waters looked so good, I threw off my shoes and jumped right in...and right freaking back out. *Holy cow! That wa-*

FORTY DAYS

ter was cold! I don't mean chilly, I mean *cold!* Later, Jarred would tell me that after just a minute or so, his feet had gone completely numb. I'm not sure he ever did get all the way in that lake.

This was perfect! It took a few attempts for me to get all the way into the water, but the lake being this cold was a blessing. Ice baths had been a big part of recovery during my training, and now I had one of the world's largest bathtubs at my disposal. It was at that point that I realized the lake was there to take care of me. Whatever I needed, she would be there. We decided right then that we would call her *Mom.*

The heat had stunted my appetite, and it was important not to get too far behind the caloric eight ball. Once back in the RV, it was time to throw on the feed bag. For the first time in two days my body temperature was normal, and all of a sudden I was starving! Mom's chilly waters had returned my appetite, and Jarred's chicken pasta was flying down. I was going lioness on that pasta, seemingly eating half my body weight. Once I finished gorging myself, the sleep fairy paid me a visit. We call it the food coma, and I was deep in it. The crew were good sports. We found a bit of shade to park the RV, and it was nap time. Mom had cooled me, fed me, and put me down for a nap. Moms are a good thing; maybe the best thing.

Day 3

It is never about where you start.
It is always about where you finish.

The delay from the prior day's nap had led to me running deep into the evening. The cooler temperatures, combined with the amazing night sky, made for a fantastic evening adventure. We were getting a later start to our third day because of that. No matter, time was a commodity we had an abundance of, time that allowed the mind to drift in many directions. Thoughts and memories that had lain dormant for so many years would suddenly jump to the front of my consciousness.

It was the most vivid memory of my childhood. I didn't remember if I had been eleven or twelve, but what I did remember was that I had been a very naive eleven or twelve. Maybe *naive* was not the best word; *innocent* was probably more accurate. From time to time, I would hear my parents argue late at night. I'm sure they thought my sister and I were fast asleep, but occasionally I would hear them. I could never tell exactly what they were arguing about. Honestly, I tried not to listen. My parents were my heroes; they weren't supposed to fight.

One day, they called my sister and me into the living room, sat us down, and told us they were getting a divorce. I didn't even know what that word meant, but I sensed that this was really a bad situation. They explained that Dad would be leaving, and my sister and I would be staying with Mom. I can't really recall much after that moment. My next memory was locking myself in the bathroom screaming at the mirror, "*Why? Why? Why?!*"

Years ago, while listening to a motivational tape by a person I no longer recall, I was struck very much by one thing he said: "Everyone, e*veryone,* has a story: *My parents got divorced, our family was impoverished, Dad was a drug addict, Mom left us, I had a learning disability, I flunked out of high school,* and so forth." He continued, "It is what we do with that story that matters."

I recently had the honor of speaking at an event with the retired four-star general, Tommy Franks. General Franks was the central commander of armed forces in the Afghan and Iraq wars. He now sits on the board of Musco Lighting, is a trustee of William Penn University, and founded the General Tommy Franks Leadership Institute, which works with the best and brightest of our high school youth. He achieved all this after he had flunked out of high school. *It ain't the cards you're dealt, it's how you play them that determines if you win or lose!*

I didn't play mine very well for many, many years. What I didn't realize then but have since come to know as truth is this: there is a gift in *every* situation. Sometimes it appears easily; other times finding it takes digging into some very messy, slimy, smelly crap that you would rather run from, but it is *always* there.

As a heartbroken eleven-year-old I was in no mood nor did I have the tools to even consider looking for a silver lining. I wasn't the least bit interested in finding the gift. All I wanted to do was run. Run from the pain; run from love; run from myself. I wanted to run as far away as I could. That running lasted nearly eleven more years and eventually almost killed me.

My sophomore year in high school, I had started experimenting with alcohol. It seemed perfect. It allowed me to run farther from my feelings, and it gave me a sense of belonging. I got good at being a drinker, at being the life of the party. It felt good. Sure, I made a few bad decisions when I was drunk, but even bad decisions somehow seemed cool. I was headed down a dangerous road and was oblivious to where it would lead. Even if I had known, I'm not sure I would have cared.

The gift, that silver lining the speaker talked about, was my mom—not the body of water this time, my actual biological mother. More specifically, the gift was my mom's unconditional love. No matter how hard I tried to self-destruct, she never failed me. She wasn't happy with the choices I was making, but she never gave up hope, never turned away. I still find it hard to understand how she held it all together, how that love never ran out.

Day 4

You have no idea what you are capable of.

"Dude, you are about to run from Chicago to Milwaukee. That's crazy!!" That was the text message I received from my niece Alyssa to start the day. She was right. That did sound crazy. If you were attempting to run ten times that far, however, it was only a stepping stone. Perspective is a weird thing. I was thankful for the message. It allowed me to take just a moment and appreciate the journey so far. I laughed a bit inside, realizing that a run to Milwaukee from Chicago had become an afterthought. *No big deal*, my subconscious had apparently decided. Three days and three marathons. *No big deal*. Really? It's amazing how our perspective, our *possible* can change as we continue to challenge ourselves.

Years ago, Team Outlaw was lining up to run their first Chicago Marathon. Team Outlaw was the running arm of our biking team, Team Bad Boy. I had begun riding with this crew of misfits years before. Team Bad Boy was not a particularly fast team. We never actually raced our bikes, even once. The bikes were not really built for speed; they were built for fun. The team roster had a wet bar bike, a grill bike, a cooler bike, and a tunes bike—complete with a generator for powering things like the blender for the wet bar. We had everything but the kitchen sink; after hearing that comment for a few years, we added a kitchen sink bike.

All of us had done some running by this point in our lives. Most had done at least one marathon. Not being interested in the status quo—just look at those bikes—we decided to take on the Chicago Marathon in a different way. We decided to turn it into a 26.2 mile celebration...a party. We rounded up a biker or two as beer support, got our cowboy hats and Team Outlaw shirts ready to go, and we were set. The game plan was simple. We would all run together, nice and easy. No person was left behind. Every six miles or so we'd find our "support" crew, jump off the road, and all share a couple beers amongst us while cheering on our fellow racers. The other runners couldn't believe it. Most of them got a real kick out of it, and a few adventurous souls stopped for a celebratory snort also. It was a blast!

As the years passed, we even convinced a bar to adopt Team Outlaw. Our first year as we ran into Chinatown we noticed a bar called the Hawkeye. Being from Iowa, there was no way we were gonna pass that up. There was no way to prove it, but I believe that may have been the first ever in-race marathon bar stop. We pulled off the course and walked right in. Once word got out in the bar what we were up to, the Outlaws were a big hit. Fifteen minutes and a few free drinks later, compliments of the bar owner, we were back to the run. Team Outlaw ran the Chicago Marathon seven or eight years in a row, and the Hawkeye became a regular stop. The owner even began welcoming us via loudspeaker.

Brian Jarchow was one of the original three Outlaws. The second year we ran, his wife, Keri, decided she was going to run along for a few miles, maybe even try to make the first beer stop. I still smile thinking about marathoning and beer stops in the same story. There were probably six or so Outlaws that second year; we had doubled our numbers. Who wouldn't want to be a part of such an adventure, spreading good will and cheer for 26.2 miles? We had perfected the five-hour fifteen-minute pace which equaled about six hours by the time you figured in our "stops". When we had finished our first stop, Kerri decided she'd tag along for a couple more miles. She was enjoying the run, and shuffling along a few more miles didn't seem too big an undertaking.

The Chicago Marathon is famous for its crowd support. People line the streets three and four deep for nearly the entire route, and they cheer on everyone. It's a giant shot in the arm for all who run. The spectators loved the Outlaws, and we had a blast tipping our cowboy hats as we acknowledged their "Go Team Outlaw!" cheers.

At mile eight it was time for Kerri to call it quits; at least that's what we thought the game plan was. She said so herself, but apparently, the smooth pace and all the fun were too much for her to call it quits just yet. Forty or so minutes later we saw our support crew and pulled over somewhere around the twelve mile mark. We cheered on our fellow runners, laughed at the confused looks on many of their faces and made a few new friends of runners and spectators alike.

Kerri was no longer just a casual joiner. Twelve miles had her headed for honorary Outlaw status. It was only the fact that she was not in official team uniform that reminded us that she was supposedly only along for a few miles. Those few miles were fast approaching the halfway mark. We left the second beer stop with Kerri still by our side. There was a valuable lesson to be learned if one was paying attention. I was paying attention. Thirteen miles turned to fourteen and fourteen turned to fifteen. Stop number three would be coming up soon. Eighteen miles. Kerri, upon reaching the stop, toasted her effort with a brewski and raised the white flag. Her couple miles had turned into eighteen. "My longest run was six miles before this," Kerri said, while enjoying her well-earned beer. We asked her when that was. "Eighth grade," she replied.

She had set out with no expectations, and that disarmed any doubts in her mind. She'd just kept plodding along with us: talking, telling stories, laughing, and playing with all the people around. There was nothing for the mind to do. No reason for it to yell at her to stop or tell her this wasn't possible. She was just a girl out for a run. Remembering the story did the same for me. It was Day Four, and I was headed for Milwaukee: just a boy out for a run.

A few short miles into the run, the skyline of Milwaukee appeared in the distance. The speech from the movie *300* blasted in my ears. "Remember us, he said to me," it began. It was an incredibly inspiring speech, and combined with the music that accompanied it, brought me to tears. It spoke of the willingness to take up the fight, no matter the odds. It detailed the sacrifice and the dedication of the *300*. I thought of all those in the cancer fight. I considered myself their warrior. This run was called "The Run to Cure Cancer." Did I believe that this journey would indeed end cancer? No. Would the money I was raising crack the code and cure all forms of this terrible disease? Probably not. Was it a fight worth taking up? Yes. Would it inspire others to follow? I hoped so.

The bike trail winding into Milwaukee was beautiful. Each city we ran into, regardless of size, brought a big surge of energy. Each was a stepping stone to finding our way back to Chicago. Milwaukee was to be busy. We had an interview with the folks from *Patch*, and a couple local folks had wanted to stop by to say *hi* and share their stories. Jarred found an industrial area near downtown that was pretty chill, parked the RV, and started making lunch. We had an hour or so until our interview and it was just a couple miles to the park where it would take place. The knock on the door took us by surprise. Jarred answered the door, and some guy on a bike asked if Steve was inside. Mike was his name. I stepped outside, introduced myself, and shook has hand. "What's going on man?" I asked, curious to find out our newest visitor's story. Mike was a volunteer firefighter in Milwaukee and a leukemia survivor, diagnosed when he was eleven. He was now forty-seven. He'd been following our journey on-line and had been on his bike all morning trying to find us. He seemed almost apologetic as he shared his story, worried that he was imposing. He must have said, "I just wanted to find you and say thanks," a dozen times. Before leaving, we asked if he would do us the favor of signing the back of the RV. He was genuinely moved doing so. Jarred and I were blown away that someone would take so much effort to seek us out.

Running through downtown Milwaukee was such an odd experience. It is hard to explain. The city was going about it's business. I was in it, passing through it, but completely separate from it. It all appeared so rigid, so machine-like, so monotonous. It was as if I were a ghost, weaving my way through ranks of people so immersed in their routine, that they noticed nothing outside of themselves. Everything was slowing down for me; I was becoming more and more aware of my surroundings and the people I passed by. It occurred to me how busy we had become, so caught up in our own routine that we passed by beauty after beauty, without so much as a pause. I was grateful to be *seeing* more in all things, to be slowing down.

The gal from *Patch* was already in the park when we arrived. Mother Nature had provided a cool, overcast day so far. It was in the low sixties, and with the breeze coming off the lake, we were actually a bit chilly. Sarah walked over and introduced herself. She was probably in her late twenties, nearly six-feet tall, and very engaging. The interview went well; I was still very much a rookie at this getting interviewed business, but she made it real easy. She had done her homework, and it seemed more a conversation than an inquisition. As we finished up, our other scheduled visitor stopped by. Jerry had emailed us the day before to find out our schedule, saying he'd like to stop by and say *hi*. We certainly were not prepared for his reasons why. Jerry has a teenage son, who early in life was diagnosed with cancer. Jerry shared with us how his son battled the disease, never losing his joy of life, no matter how tough the treatments got. He told of bone marrow transplants, eventual remission, and a recurrence that led to his son having his arm amputated. You could hear the disbelief in his voice when he spoke of how his son still remains a kid full of enthusiasm and joy. You got the feeling it was his son supporting him through the journey. He told us he felt it necessary to find us and say thanks, that his son wanted to be here but was in treatment. Jerry would be heading back to the hospital after he left us.

Running out of Milwaukee later that afternoon, I reminisced

FORTY DAYS

to the start of the day and the speech that I had replayed over and over. "Remember us," it had said. I would never forget the people we met that day. Real heroes. True warriors.

Day 5

Take a kid for a walk.

My sister Kristan is four years younger than me, and our relationship is one of the great joys of my life. We talk every week, sometimes every day. She has a great sense of humor and is just smart enough to realize the comedic genius that I am. She and Michael, who ran with me on that inferno of a Day One, have three children. Sarah (Boo) is their oldest, followed by Alyssa (Lyss), and Thomas (Hubba), their youngest.

I often joke that I entered my first race in Manitou Springs as a way to meet chicks. I'm now forty-six and still single. *How'd that work out for me?* I have been so fortunate to be a part of those three kids' lives. Being an uncle is a great thing, and I love it. They've dubbed me the "Funcle." *How cool is that?*

My Aunt Barbara was for me the female version of the *funcle* I was for those kids. Growing up as a city kid hadn't provided me with many opportunities for outdoor activities or exploring wild places. Barbara took time one spring afternoon to take me on my first real adventure, and she has always held a special place in my heart.

My mother came from a big family, with seven brothers and sisters. Her sister Barbara was married to Uncle Raymond, and they lived on a farm outside of Rolfe, Iowa. *I dare you to try and find that on a map.* It was a great place to visit. Barbara and Raymond had five kids, motorbikes, fireworks, wild animals, and big loud parties that seemed to be one never ending laugh. That house was so much fun, so full of joy. It was a special place.

I loved the farm too. There was so much going on. We were rarely indoors; we had too much to do outside. There were pigs to check on and chickens to bother. A giant rope hung from one of the oaks with a car tire at the end of it; that thing could keep us busy for hours! It was a never-ending playground for a city kid.

One spring morning Aunt Barbara invited me to go on an adventure. Just me, no one else was allowed. We packed a big lunch; there was always great food at the farm. We grabbed a blanket to sit on and headed out. I felt so special to be Aunt Barbara's only sidekick that day. The walk was probably only a mile or so to get to the other side of the farm, but because it was my first hike ever, it seemed much longer.

Finally, we crossed the last fence, and we laid our blanket on the ground. The view was fantastic; from our vantage point, the whole valley opened up in front of us, dotted by quite a few cows roaming around. Aunt Barbara unpacked our basket and began to tell me why we were there; springtime on the farm meant it was time for calves to be born. Aunt Barbara said, "Pay attention. Look for any cows that have separated themselves and gone off to be alone."

Steven Cannon

"Why?" I asked. She explained that when a momma cow is ready to give birth, she'll want to be by herself. *Wow!* I thought. "You mean we are here to watch a baby cow be born?" This was big stuff.

Aunt Barbara said that yes, indeed, we were here to see if any of the momma cows were ready and if so to make sure things went okay. I scanned the valley, hoping to find a cow that was noticeably away from the rest. I desperately wanted to find one so I could impress Aunt Barbara that she'd made a great choice in an adventure partner. I pointed out a few that turned out to be duds, but then after a few missed calls, I asked, "How about that one over there?"

"That one does look like she may be getting ready," Aunt Barbara agreed. She said we should keep an eye on her. There was nothing in the world that could have taken my eyes off that cow.

Each time she moved, I'd whisper as loudly as I could, "Aunt Barbara, Aunt Barbara, look, look!" And each time she'd tell me to keep watching, keep an eye on her. Then it actually began to happen. Aunt Barbara perked right up. As we sat there together on that hillside, that cow gave birth to a calf. I was in awe.

As soon as we got back to the farmhouse, I started jabbering. "Mom, Uncle Raymond, you wouldn't believe it...it happened... there was this cow...I saw it first...it had gone off by itself 'cause that's what cows do when they have babies...I showed Aunt Barbara where it was....and then this happened...and then...and then!" It still remains one of the great memories of my childhood.

Aunt Barbara died from cancer at the young age of forty-four. Today, Day Five, was the thirty-first anniversary of her death. It would be my day to take her on an adventure; she would run a marathon with me. I imagined her saying to all her friends in heaven, "It was amazing, we ran along the lake, and through the woods...and we met this person and that person...and when it got too hot we jumped in the lake...and then...and then!"

Thanks, Aunt Barbara. You live on because of the day we shared on that hillside together. I love you.

Day 6

When everything inside you says stop, that is the moment you must press on.

The excitement from the first couple days of running felt so far behind me. My longest training weeks for this adventure had been around 100 miles. During those weeks, my coach would have me stack two, sometime three twenty-plus mile runs in a row. There is a fine balance in training for multi-day runs. One must push the long days as far as possible and as many in a row as one can, without completely breaking down the body. It is very similar to training for your first marathon. You want to get in as many long runs as you can without blowing yourself up. I wasn't going to run forty marathons in a row during training any more than you would run five or ten marathons during your marathon training.

Pushing yourself through training not only sharpens you physically, it also sharpens you mentally. You run the first twenty miles of a marathon with your body. You run the last six miles and 385 yards with your soul. It is somewhere around that twenty-mile mark, the "wall," that the mind begins to scream *Enough is enough!* I love distance running or distance anything because it unifies. We all take the same journey, just at different speeds. When you cross that finish line you share a bond with all your fellow racers. Nothing needs to be said; it is just known that all of you went to a dark place and willed yourself through to the other side. It is a feeling that can be partially explained but can only fully be understood by doing. Once you make that journey, you are changed forever.

Ultras and multi-day runs are no different. The journey is the same; the clock just runs a bit longer. When I was running across Iowa in 2009, there were incredibly intense moments early on where, for reasons unknown, I would just start crying. It was the oddest thing. There were no thoughts that were triggering these emotional outbursts. I wasn't listening to Barbara Streisand or tuning into Tony Robbins. I was just shuffling along and *Waaaaah!* The outburst never lasted long and was always followed by an incredible sense of relief. I believe that the running, because of its intense physical demands, was stripping me bare. Each mile peeled away a layer until, sooner or later, it uncovered something that I had buried long ago. Like an oil gusher, it would just explode out of me, so glad to be free. At first, I felt embarrassed by these moments; later, I came to welcome them. I always felt so good afterwards, somehow lighter on my feet.

That run across Iowa marked the first time I had attempted so many marathons in a row. Eleven days, eleven marathons was what it took to get from the Missouri River to the mighty Mississippi. Each day became a new personal best and a new chance to go deeper inside myself. Day Seven of that run was the day that stood out the most in my memories; it was the day that my body, so controlled by the mind, said *Enough is enough*. This was no quick sob-and-move-on-lighter-and-happier. The best I can describe the experience was a running version of a mental breakdown. Everything got very dark and very slow: seemingly one thing after another started shutting down. Like the marathon wall, I had to learn to run with my soul to get through it, turning off the signals from both the body and mind.

I knew from my Iowa run that the wall was out there waiting for me. The difference now was that I ran with Lake Michigan, *Mom,* by my side, so I looked forward to it. I knew what was waiting on the other side. Peace, ease, rhythm, flow. Over 130 miles were behind me now. During training, I ran almost exclusively on trails and dirt roads. The asphalt jungle is a body wrecker; it should be outlawed. I had put in many months and thousands of miles with no major injuries, and I know it is because I stayed off the hard stuff. The first five days of this run had been nothing but the hard stuff, and my legs were revolting. The discomfort was made bearable because the voices in my head drowned out the pain. Like a kid being ignored, each day my mind got more and more upset, yelling at me with greater frequency. Today it was nonstop. All the signs were there. I knew where this was heading...into the dark place. The real dark place. The place where the bad people live.

As the sun began to set on Day Six, somewhere around the twenty mile mark, I spotted the RV just up ahead. I had never hated running so much in my life. One negative thought after another filled my head. Every self-doubting voice and sentiment you could ever imagine was running through me. It was a feeling of desperation. The temptation to quit, just to quiet the voices and make it all stop, would not let me go. The bad people were relentless, strong in their resolve. All they requested of me was to stop fighting; if I did so, gave up, they promised the pain would end.

Normally, Jarred and I would chat about something at each stop. We are the best of friends, and conversation almost always comes quite naturally. Not now. I told him what was happening, and he understood, having been with me in 2009. I told him the pace was gonna get real slow but not to worry; I'd get there. Nothing else was said. I put my earphones in, not to listen to music but to muffle any outside noise. I wanted to go into the hole as deeply as I could. I wanted to experience it fully.

If you have never run beyond what you thought you were capable of, be it a 5k, 10k, marathon or longer, this may seem hard to understand. I had run nearly six marathons to get here. I wasn't gonna blast music and try and run around it or run from it. I was going into it and through it. Almost immediately, it started to happen. The voices in my head were loud, yet they really didn't *say* anything, they just conveyed a sense of sadness, doubt and desperation, a sense that it was over, that this was impossible for me, that I would fail. I would not allow the thoughts to take me; I would accept them, let them keep coming, remain unattached. *Breathe. Breathe. Breathe.*

My pace was barely faster than a walk, but that was of little consequence. This had nothing to do with time. I was entering into a place of no time, a place where—if I could let it all go and if I could continue deeper and deeper into the hole—I would disappear. I would no longer be separate from the lake, or the countryside, or the pavement that had been beating me. I would become one with it. Connected. In the flow.

Steven Cannon

Tears began flowing down my face, and my breath was broken up by sobs. If you allow it, passing through the dark place becomes an out-of-body experience. You literally run out of your mind. There is a huge pull to stop, to return to safety, but there is no real safety in doing so. The safety lies just beyond where you think you are capable of going. That is the place where you find connection to the best of who you can be. You tap into the flow. You become part of everything and nothing.

The day was done. I have no idea how long those last miles took. I stumbled into the RV completely empty. *Completely empty.* The run would begin anew tomorrow.

Day 7

Follow your heart. Please!

My definition of a hero is a person who, through their actions, inspires you to be the best you can be. Later in my life, I appreciated and was profoundly affected by my mother as well as my Grandpa Bill and his wife, Rachel. I am where I am and who I am due to these three extraordinary people. They always kept the faith.

My first hero? I don't remember having many heroes as a young kid. The first people I can remember looking up to were sports figures. Boxing was very popular when I was growing up. There was no pay-per-view then. The big fights were on ABC and available to all. The early seventies and eighties were the glory years for boxing. Muhammad Ali was nearing the end of his career, but he was still bigger than life, a huge personality, and my first inspirational hero. I had no intentions of ever being a boxer, but Ali transcended boxing. He was and still is regarded as "the greatest of all time."

Steven Cannon

As I grew up, basketball became my sport of choice. There was a small community college in Burlington, Iowa, where we lived. My dad took me to the games, and I fell in love with them. The seventies were the domain of "Dr. J." Julius Erving was as much a ballet dancer as a basketball player. Like Ali, he was bigger than the game. He transcended it. You would watch games for that moment, that one play, where the unreal became real. Like the Ali shuffle, Dr. J also had his moves. There were times he would leave the ground and seemingly stay in the air forever. These athletes made us believe that we could be great because they were great.

Later, in my twenties, I found new heroes. They were not well known like Ali or Dr. J; they were adventure athletes: people like Marshall Ulrich, Ian Adamson, Rebecca Rusch, Ray Zahab, Lisa Tamati, Terry Fox and Lisa Smith Batchen. Their accomplishments are far too many to list. They are legends. A part of this run belonged to each of them.

I was living in Iowa City (*Go Hawks!*) in the early nineties. Ty Dickerson, a friend from college, had started rock climbing. There were not a lot of mountains in Iowa, and at that time there weren't too many rock climbers either. The University of Iowa had an indoor climbing wall, and Ty had started hitting it regularly and asked me along. Some people know from an early age that adventure is going to be their life, be it camping, hiking, climbing, surfing, or flying. I was not one of those people. Apparently, the spirit of adventure was hiding in me somewhere, as I was drawn to rock climbing. I fell in love with it, and it opened all the doors that have led me to where I am now.

Ty and I started hitting other indoor climbing gyms around Iowa as well. It was nothing for us to drive an hour to the Quad Cities to climb new indoor routes. I'd lay awake at night, working through moves in my head on a particular section of a route that was giving me trouble. Soon we were grabbing guidebooks and looking for state parks that had climbable rock. It turned out there were actually a few places in Iowa that offered great climbing, and in Illinois too.

Those trips fueled our desire to head west; Eldorado Canyon in Colorado was one of the hottest spots for climbing. Like so many climbers that preceded us, its call was too much to resist. We decided we'd load up Ty's VW van and go for it; it would be the first big adventure trip for me. We had damn little money, but all we needed was enough gas to get there and back, a few bucks for ramen noodles, and we'd be in heaven. It became a classic dirt bagger adventure, just like the ones I had read about prior to our leaving. We climbed all day and read about big wall climbers like John Wall as we sat up in our tents at night. I had never seen the Rockies before that trip, and I can still remember the thrill as I saw their peaks rise in the distance for the first time, over twenty years ago. The mountains are a magical place; if they get hold of your soul they never let go. I knew as we left Colorado, the Rockies now in our rear view mirror, that I would return.

It would only take a few years until the tall snow-capped peaks called me back. Work had thrown me a curve ball; I had started a business not long after college, and after a few somewhat successful years, my biggest client eliminated the need for my services. Just like that I was at a crossroads. A buddy of Ty's and mine, Jon Madsen AKA Maddog, had been living in Colorado for a few years and also had been bitten by the climbing bug. He managed a running store, which was not much of a big deal to me as I had *no* interest in *ever* being a runner. I was however interested in getting a hold of more rock. Maddog and I spent an hour or so on the phone, and a couple days later the trip was on. I had a really well-thought-out plan. I'd take what money I had in the bank, head to Colorado, climb rock, camp, and explore until it ran out. I'd figure out the rest then. Without knowing it, I was putting a trust in the universe that if I took a few steps to follow my dreams, perhaps it would open doors to support me.

You often hear people say, "I wish I could do that," or "I wish I could do this." Well, you can. You just choose to, and you go do it. The rest will take care of itself. Colorado changed the course of my life in ways I would have never imagined and for which I am incredibly thankful. I do not even want to think of how different my life would be now had I not loaded up the truck and what little I had and headed west.

Day 8

Not every bandana lives happily ever after.

Stay In the moment. It is a lesson learned in distance running. There were thirty-three days remaining before I was to return to the exact place where I'd taken the first step of this run. To spend even an instant contemplating 850 more miles, the next day, or even just the end of the current day was an invitation for the mind to obsess. Two nights prior I had broken my mind by ignoring its incessant cries to stop, broken it to the point that it gave up. Thinking about days or miles into the future would reawaken its cries, and that was something I did not want to invite.

Running has taught me many lessons and introduced me to many teachers. The physical side of running is no longer as interesting as the spiritual. It no longer matters how far I can go outside, but rather how far I can go inside. It has become a form of meditation, a practice.

Dream big. We are not meant to live small lives. We are born to

Steven Cannon

be giants, and the universe is here to support each of us in this endeavor of hugeness. It is through dreaming big that all the wheels get put into motion, including fear. Fear is a fraud, a ghost, a mirage. It certainly appears real, and the more we allow it to hang around, the larger it can grow until it becomes a giant dream-killer. Given the opportunity, it will start firing rapidly, telling you all the things that could go wrong and the reasons you couldn't, shouldn't, or can't.

Here are a few quotes from my fear monster: "Nobody has ever run around Lake Michigan. What makes you think you can? You barely made it across Iowa in eleven days, now you think you can run the equivalent of crossing Iowa three times...in a row? Who's gonna drive, who's gonna sponsor you, what if all the roads don't have shoulders to run on?" My "other" brain would fire back... "*Enough!* Shut the hell up! Get back to the task at hand!" Imagine that incessant chatter dancing in your head for months.

Stay in the moment. You can't run mile 732 until you have run mile 731. Fear leads to inaction. Ask yourself how many *Aha!* or *Eureka!* ideas you have let drift away on a boat captained by fear. Remember this. There is always someone sitting on the sidelines screaming it can't be done, while someone just like you goes ahead and does it.

This is not to say that one can just show up untrained in Chicago with a pair of socks and shoes and expect to succeed, although, that person has a hell of a lot better chance than the one who listens to fear and never even tries. Chadd Konig, who paddled on a surf board from Santa Cruz to Santa Barbara California said, "No matter how carefully you prepare, something will always go wrong, and that is when it gets wild and free. Those are the moments that allow

43

you to truly see within yourself." *Exactly.*

Once I announced the attempt to run around Lake Michigan, folks went question-crazy. What about this? And this? And that? And this? Almost none of what they asked was important. We needed a support vehicle, a driver, gas for said vehicle, food and six pairs of running shoes. Would I pay attention to other details and do my absolute best to ensure success? Absolutely. I made sure to knock these details out one by one, staying in the moment, and whenever fear started its rapid-fire games, I would return to the basics, knowing I was okay.

Trust that there is a greatness in you that is beyond what you can see for yourself. We have all heard the statistics about using only ten percent of our brain. It is true. We are all capable of so much more than we realize. If we all stayed in that space of tackling only what we knew we were capable of, how damn boring that would be! Don't fear fear, use it. Use it as a sign that you are reaching beyond your comfort zone. Embrace it. Fear hates hugs. It feeds off itself. The more you push it away the stronger it becomes. Eventually you will welcome it and watch it become weak and powerless.

It was the start of Day Eight. *How would I possibly get through another thirty-three days, or even another 26.2 miles again today? If I didn't start eating better, I would be screwed. God, I hope my legs don't hurt like this all day long.* Nope, that recording was not welcome. I knew I could take one step. I'd start with that.

Lake Michigan was the most wonderful of running companions; she possessed so many amazing traits. Most days, I only needed glance to my right, and her immense size and beauty instantly inspired. No matter the extreme temperature of the day, a breeze of some sort provided relief from the seemingly endless heat wave.

Steven Cannon

Her frigid waters brought down my temperature during the day, allowing my appetite to return. At day's end, those same waters served as Mother Nature's version of an ice bath, taking away not only my breath but also the pain of the day.

Door County also provided inspiration to move forward. Everyone has a place or two in this country that they claim to be the most beautiful, beyond words. We had referred to Door County as "the armpit," because it sort of looked like that on the map. Never had such a beautiful place been given such an unflattering nickname. Neither Jarred or I had ever been there. Everyone we had spoken to before the run had said "You ain't gonna believe how beautiful Door County is." For the next four days it was our running playground. Door County lays claim to 300 miles of shoreline, five magnificent state parks and eleven lighthouses. Each step built on the next, leading to one mile then two. The magnificence of this place provided more than enough motivation to continue on. I imagined myself a running Shackleton or Marco Polo.

Jarred had provided me with a brand new bandana to start the day. It was a nice little present. I always wore one tied around my neck. It was multi-functional. It could be used to just soak up sweat or wipe my face from time to time. Jarred would almost always soak it in cold water at the start of each running leg. During the hottest of times he'd fill it with ice and roll it up, in an attempt to keep my temperature out of the red zone. It would take my breath away as he put it on my neck. Many times, by the time I finished a couple miles and was returning to the RV, it would be bone dry.

Before starting the day, I had noticed a sweet triathlon-bike locked to the pole not far off the road in the park we found ourselves in. *Perhaps I'd find a running companion on my travels this morning.* It was not long into the day when that exact thing happened. Rachel was training for an upcoming event. She shared that often she chose this place to train because of its hills and seldom-used trails. Rachel was one fit lady and, had she not been so intrigued by what I had going on, would not have been shuffling along at the pace I required. I let her know that if she didn't mind the pace I'd love to check out the trails she spoke of. Every chance I got to run on the dirt, I took. The single-track trails were perfect, forgiving to the legs, and the constant turns and occasional tree roots kept the mind occupied. I delighted in the company of my new friend and our shared running adventure. Our detour however, meant that I had been out on the run longer than normal. If not for the rumbling in my stomach, this would not have been a problem. It was quickly becoming a real issue. Although my trail partner and I were getting along swimmingly, it did not seem to me that our relationship had reached a level of intimacy that I could just give her a shout relating to my predicament. Hoping she would just run ahead, I let her know I needed a quick bathroom break. She let me know it was no problem. She was fine with me ducking behind the tree while she waited. As she stood a mere ten feet away and showed no signs of moving, I realized more information needed to be shared. "Gonna be a little more than just a quick pit stop." Quickly realizing my predicament she laughed and headed down the trail, giving me adequate space for all eventualities. She couldn't get out of there soon enough. My situation was a full on emergency by now. So much so, that it was not until after resolving the situation, shorts still around my ankles, I realized I had not packed tissues of any sort. It only took a few minutes to catch back up with my trail-running friend. She jokingly asked if everything had come out all right. I assured her that all things were once again right with the world. She was a good sport and got a good laugh out of my reference to the trail grenade that had been buried not far behind us. I hoped Jarred would be so understanding, as his recently gifted Bandana had just paid the ultimate price. On a more positive note, I still had both of my socks.

The day became less and less about twenty-six miles and more and more about how deeply we could immerse ourselves in this beautiful place. Rachel gave us directions how we should best exit the park to continue on. We shared a big hug and wished each other well. She took a moment to sign the back of the RV, adding her name to those who had shared time with us and made the adventure so much richer. Many of these people I would never see again, but their faces and their spirit would remain with me always.

Hours later, just before exiting the park, we came upon an immense fire tower. This thing was like a skyscraper. It had to be a couple hundred feet to the top, with the stairs and the structure growing more and more compressed as you reached it. The giant structure also sat atop the highest point in the park, just a few feet from a cliff's edge. Lake Michigan was easily 500 feet or more below. I am not normally afraid of heights. I've jumped out of planes and rappelled off everything from a cliff's edge to a grain silo. For some reason, ascending this sucker had me spooked. The combination of how small the structure was at the top, combined with the exposure, had me on my hands and knees the last few sections. No lie, I was crawling, stopping at each turn, having to talk myself into continuing. It took me close to ten minutes to get up the last twenty feet or so. Once on the way-too-small-for-comfort top deck, I still could not bring myself to stand up. The view was insane. It felt as if I was thousands of feet above the lake on that small perch. The railings made it difficult to get good pictures, so there I was on my knees trying to reach up over them in an attempt to get good shots. I'd snap a picture, crouch back down, catch my breath, check it out, and retake until I had a winner or two. The incredible beauty at my disposal was not nearly enough to get my scared ass to stand up. There was no way in hell that was happening. Without a climbing harness or parachute, I realized at that moment, I was quite a sissy. Eventually, convinced my photos were good enough, I slinked back down the stairs until I felt secure enough to actually stand up and walk back to the safety of the earth. The remaining miles slowly descended from the park, eventually placing us back alongside the great lake. It had been a very eventful day, full of adventure. As I ended the day soaking in *Mom's* healing waters, there was no dread of the upcoming day, no fear of what could go wrong, but rather an excitement as to what awaited.

Day 9

One step at a time

How does one go about eating an elephant? Accomplishing anything big happens by accomplishing a lot of things small. I could not take a single 1,037-mile-long step. I could however take one small step many, many, many times in a row. I love numbers. With all things, it is important to have a game plan and know what is ahead of you. My stride is about three feet, give or take. That's pretty much equal to a meter. There are about 1,600 meters in a mile.

I figure, for ease of math, that I'll be closer to two thousand steps per mile; when I get into multi-day mode, there is not much striding going on. Efficiency is the name of the game, and a shorter stride length equals less bounce, which equals less wear and tear. Another bonus is that two thousand is a nice even number. Two thousand strides per mile and twenty-six miles or so per day equals fifty-two thousand steps per day. My journey should take me forty days. Are you ready for this number?

FORTY DAYS

That's 2,080,000 steps.

Ask yourself, "Can I take one step?" We are no longer necessarily speaking about running. Place your own word or goal in here. What's your dream? Do you want to be a better husband, wife, parent or friend? Can you take one step in that direction? Just one step? You're damn right you can. Do you want to start your own business or nonprofit? Do you want to walk the Great Wall or step on a surfboard just once? Can you take one step in that direction? Absolutely you can. Now what? Can you take another step? Just one more? No doubt about it. Each step you take makes the next step possible. Worrying about step 2,080,000 at step 80,145 is silly. You start right where you are, with just one step. Enjoy it, be in it, and then take step two, knowing all along where you are headed. Compare yourself to no one else! It is *your* journey.

How do you eat an elephant?

One bite at a time.

Day 10

Every step leads somewhere...

The fall colors had been in full bloom on a day twenty-two years ago. The trees painted the skyline with shades of yellows, browns, and reds. There were two other colors that also signified that fall had arrived in Iowa City: black and gold, the colors of the University of Iowa Hawkeyes. I had graduated from Iowa in 1988 with a major in communications and a minor in partying. Actually, it may have been the other way around. Looking back on it, it was clear that I missed out on much of the college experience due to too much time with a beer in my hand.

Alcoholism is a sneaky disease. It is not like most of our other diseases. It is difficult to quantify. One thing is easy to quantify: Alcohol is a poison. Drink enough of it, and it will kill you. That can happen on a one-night binge, getting behind the wheel when drunk, or slowly over time. It can start with the occasional social drink, wanting to fit in, and can develop into a habit that slowly steals your soul.

I began my drinking career as a sophomore in high school on a random Saturday night that eventually landed me back on my front porch and puking my guts out for twenty-four hours or so. The following Monday, my efforts had gained me attention in school, which seemed to make it pretty cool. Weekend binges soon became the norm. Drinking let me fit in and gave me "friends" who liked to do the same. The list of stupid things I did while drunk is too long to enumerate, but it's safe to say that I could have easily been one of those meaningless deaths due to drinking as a youngster. I cannot imagine the worry I put those closest to me through. This much is certain: my grades, my athletics, and my development as a person all were affected. I was headed down a road to nowhere.

College. I was nineteen years old and legal! This was heaven. I could make as many poor decisions as I wanted with no parents to answer to. I could stay out way too late, drink way too much, miss as many classes as I wanted, and get absolutely no exercise. Like I said, *Heaven.*

"You have two choices, son," my step dad said as we discussed my midterm report card of three F's and a C. "You get those grades up or your ass is headed for the military." Message received. No way was I going to leave this wonderful place. By semester's end I had managed all C's. I was back in business.

I was hungry to belong, to be accepted. Partying and drinking gave me that. A huge void had been created when my parents divorced. I didn't realize it at the time, but I was attempting to fill that hole, that desire to be loved, through drinking.

"What seems to be the problem, officer?" I asked after pulling into the bar parking lot. "Do you realize you've been going the

Steven Cannon

wrong way on a one way street, son? Could we have you step out of the car please?" The sobriety tests didn't go well. I cried like a baby as they booked me into jail. I was smashed; I registered over two times the legal limit, a number my buddies and I would later celebrate. To think of that now makes me sick. My soul was slowly being put to sleep by the booze.

I quit drinking for a couple weeks to prove that I didn't have a drinking problem. Then I decided that since I didn't have a drinking problem I would just have a few during our five or six nights on the town each week. Once I realized I could handle that, then it was okay to let go of the reins and kick 'em back full speed. I just wouldn't drive, which of course I would eventually do as well. That is the deceptive beauty of alcohol. It corrupts slowly. One small wrong step at a time was taking me to a place so far away, I would be unrecognizable to myself.

It was tailgate time, 8 a.m. on a beautiful Saturday morning, and perfect football weather. The beers were beginning to flow freely. It had been years since I'd earned my first drunk driving conviction driving the wrong way on the one-way street. I knew I was drinking too much, but I didn't have the guts to ask for help. It had become easier to just go with it. Drinking had become my escape from the drinking. I was trapped in a place of my own creation. *How did I get here?* One wrong step a time, taken many, many times over. I couldn't even see back to where it all started. It was too far away.

I had seventy-five miles to drive. The party was over. I had not had a drink for an hour or so. Never mind the endless drinks since that morning; I was fine. It was mostly interstate highway back to Waterloo. If I could get out of Iowa City undetected, I'd be home free.

FORTY DAYS

I had never given much thought to angels, guardian or otherwise, until that night. Had I made it to the interstate that fall evening I would have died. Or worse, I would have killed others in the process. Two years earlier, my best friend Brian "Reggie" Hammond had died in a winter automobile accident. No one was at fault. His car crossed the center lane due to icy roads and hit a semi truck traveling the other way. He was thrown from the vehicle right in front of a nursing home. They were unable to save him. I miss him every single day. I know in my heart he saved my life that night.

The red flashing lights in my rear view mirror did not evoke feelings of dread or fear, as they had years before. I let out a sigh of relief, slowly pulled the car over and welcomed the officer. I can only imagine his confusion as I thanked him for stopping me. I let him know there was no reason to go through all the sobriety tests, which he informed me had to be done. I didn't pass a single one, and I'm sure the breathalyzer confirmed why. He read me my rights, handcuffed me, and put me into his vehicle. There was a surreal clarity to the moment, considering my level of intoxication. I said a silent "thank you" to my guardian angel. Reggie had stepped in and saved my life. There was no doubt in my mind. It was at that point I began the long trek to find myself. One step at a time.

Day 11

The power of one thought

We were in the heart of Door County. The past couple days had been spectacular. A small roadside park had been our campsite the previous night. Exiting the RV, we followed the trail markers directing us to a scenic view area. It was worth the hobble and provided a breathtaking view of Lake Michigan, hundreds of feet below. There could be no better place to begin the day. Washington Island was just off in the distance. I allowed my gaze to drift further north. Although beyond view, I knew the upper peninsula of Michigan was there, waiting. It filled me with wonder, knowing that not so many days later, I would find myself in that place, being able to look south to this place. This was not the type of place to just run through. Staying in this area for days would be preferred. The thought certainly crossed my mind a few times. I'm sure others before me simply chose never to leave and now call Door County home.

FORTY DAYS

This was to be a very exciting day. I had never strung more than eleven marathons back to back to back to back...to back. If today was a success, tomorrow I would get the chance to do so. A single thought, if it is the right thought, can carry you through your entire day. I was becoming a master of this game. It created purpose which in turn created drive and excitement. It also kept me in the moment. "Finish Day Eleven, and you get to take a shot at a new best for yourself, Day Twelve," I told myself. My mind was right. The day was done before it even started. I would see Day Twelve. I was sure of it.

Does a person find his destiny, his purpose, and his passion, or do they find him? I think that it can be both. There are those who tell stories of their youth, of reading books about great adventurers, knowing from a very early age that would be their path. Others are blown off course almost immediately. It could be a divorce or perhaps they are born into such desperate circumstances that they are unable to see beyond the basic needs for survival, never to discover their true path.

I believe that each of us is born to excel. We are made to live giant, exciting, passionate lives. I also believe that many of us ignore that call, instead choosing to follow society's path. There is a problem with the second option. It leaves us hollow, unfulfilled. This much I know: every single person who follows their dreams and listens to their own unique inner voice wins. Do what you love, and you will succeed. It is a universal law, and it never fails. It puts us in the flow, and all that is needed manifests. Each and every one of us has a unique gift, a greatness inside. Honor that. Go for that. When your last day is done, make sure the movie that passes before your eyes is worth watching.

Day 12

Stupid, stupid, stupid.

Each step I took from this day forward would be a new personal best for me. In 2009 I'd taken on my home state of Iowa by foot. That journey covered 292 miles, the equivalent of a marathon each day for eleven days. It was now Day Twelve. Everything had gone pretty much as expected up to this point. My body was becoming accustomed to the distance each day. The big emotional breakdown was now behind me, and the peace that followed provided a welcome companion. Day Twelve, however, interrupted that peace a bit. This was uncharted territory.

Many questions and thoughts had been attempting to engage my mind. When your sole reason for being is to run day after day, the mind becomes unnecessary. Once you have successfully tucked it into bed, and it is sleeping quietly, it is best not to wake it. The mind can be very cranky if its slumber is interrupted.

"Can you keep this up?"

FORTY DAYS

"You've never run more than 300 miles."
"Will there be more emotional revolts?"
"How long will this heat wave last?"
"Waaaaaah!"

The baby was awake and would need some tender loving care to get back to sleep.

Running had become for me as much a spiritual experience as a physical one over the past years. Running offered so much more than physical benefits. If I get out and move, the physical, healthy benefits take care of themselves. If I take time to look beyond the physical, there is an opportunity to turn running into a much deeper, all-encompassing activity. There were twenty-six miles waiting for me. A marathon would give me plenty of time to rock my mind back to sleep.

I began reading and studying *The Book of Secrets* by Osho many years ago. *The Book of Secrets* contains over 100 meditations. Osho is known for his *dynamic meditation.* I had always held a vision of meditation as someone in a quiet space, sitting motionless and alone. Dynamic meditation uses motion, action, almost a "crazy dance" to shake off the unreal, leaving only the real, the quiet, in its place. It is then that you can access peace and your quiet self.

Running became my dynamic meditation. Much like attempting to sit quietly while the mind screams for its daily dose of noise, running multiple marathons had the same effect. The mind did not resist at first, but with each passing day devoid of computers, voice mails and traffic jams, it grew more and more restless. I was taking away the baby's toys. The physical activity, the pushing beyond the mind, allows you to eventually find the space. The space is difficult to describe; however you will know it once you access it. Once you access it, you will yearn to stay in it.

Running was once again my vehicle. Not a vehicle to take me on the remaining 700 miles of the physical journey. As long as I kept moving, the miles would take care of themselves. Running was a vehicle to lose the false and gain the real. Twenty-six miles lay ahead, twenty-six miles to find more of myself and give back to all those in the cancer fight. My feet began slowly to shuffle along. The mind began slowly to nod off. *Peace restored,* or so I thought.

Everything had seemed under control. Then, the next thing I knew, I was in Lake Michigan, sitting in water up to my waist. I had been unable to walk the few steps from the RV to her healing waters on my own; my right leg was nearly useless below me. All this happened because of a brief lapse of sanity.

Thirty minutes or so earlier, I had approached the RV and broken a cardinal rule. I had let myself think that this was the end of the day. I very seldom asked Jarred for updates on how far we had to go. I did this for two reasons. One, I didn't want to know; I enjoyed getting lost in the run. Two, it sucked hearing twenty miles to go, eighteen miles to go, and so on. I'd rather stay in the moment, eat when I was hungry, rest when I was tired, and when we were done for the day, Jarred would tell me.

I was tired, and I had wanted it to be the end of the day. It wasn't. It had been a false summit created in my mind. I'd let myself believe this had to be the end, and when it wasn't, I lost that sense of peace. I was certain Jarred didn't want to see me finish and had become jealous of all the attention I was getting. "Two more miles," *you say?* "Don't think I can handle it," *you say?* "Think you can break me," *you say?* "You just try to keep up asshole." All these thoughts went through my head as I grabbed one more water bottle, slammed the RV door, and took off at a full sprint. I was going to bury these last two miles that, in my mind, I wasn't even supposed to run, and I was going to teach Jarred once and for all that there was no stopping me. A mile and a half down the road, my right leg blew. The pain almost knocked me off my feet. The last half mile was done on one leg.

Jarred's look said all that I was thinking. *What the hell happened?! What could I possibly have been thinking?! Why the stupid sprint?! Had I just thrown away all the training and effort of the past years in just two miles?* How could I possibly hope to knock out 26.2 miles tomorrow, let alone twenty-eight more marathons, on a right leg that I could barely walk on? The shooting pains that accompanied putting any weight on my right leg were debilitating. Jarred helped me into the lake, and I soaked in Mom's hopefully healing waters, disgusted with myself. I stood, hoping the soak and the short rest had helped. It had not. I threw my arm over Jarred's shoulder. He pretty much carried me from the lake back into the RV.

Top Left: Best Kiss of the Run
Top Right: My Happiest Place? On Any Adventure
Bottom: 100 Degrees Couldn't Stop These Friends (Day 39
Indiana Dunes)

Top: My Des Moines Family
Bottom: From One Extreme to the Other
(Minus 10 at the Tuscobia 150)

Top: End of Run Across Iowa in a Bit of Disbelief
Bottom: The Race That Almost Ended Me
(The World's Longest Kayak Race – The Yukon River Quest)

Day 13

Uncertainty is a part of every worthwhile journey.

It had proved to be a very anxious night of sleep. Sleep, in general, was difficult when I was on a run. I would typically pass out quickly, sleep very hard for an hour or two, and then wake up in a pool of my own sweat. The temperature in the RV was in the mid sixties every night, sometimes even colder. Jarred and I would joke at night that you could hang meat in there. No matter, my body was cooking from the inside out.

Marshall Ulrich commented in his book, *Running on Empty*, that there were times his wife was awakened by him running in his sleep. His body simply could not shut off. He was running nearly sixty miles a day, sometimes eighteen hours or more. I wasn't near that, but I could relate, in that my body could not lay still for more than a few hours without needing to reposition. It was trying to recover as best it could. On any of the previous twelve nights, I would have just rolled over, found a comfortable position, passed back out, and repeated the routine every few hours.

Not this night. I woke up from a bad dream that the run was over. I dreamt that the damage to my leg had stopped me, and my momentary loss of sanity had cost me my shot of seeing Chicago twenty-eight days from now. Waking up didn't provide much relief, as I still did not know if *Mom's* healing waters or my bartering with every god and guardian angel of running I could think of would pay off. I took a quick inventory by moving the leg a bit, not wanting to really test it. There was no shooting pain, and that was good enough for me. Hope is the best of things. I drifted off hoping for happier dreams.

The toughest part of every day was the three steps from the edge of the bed to the toilet. If I could make that, I could move to step two and change my clothes. If I could do that, I could slowly walk the seven steps to the front of the RV and sit down for breakfast. This routine held even more importance this morning because it was entirely possible that I might not make those first three steps.

Nice and easy, buddy, I remember thinking, as I took a few extra minutes to gather myself at the edge of the bed. These first steps were always a bit dangerous with the plantar fasciitis in both feet. Patience was so important. I knew from experience that if I could get my butt out the door and walk a mile or so, everything would start to warm up, and the day would be possible. This leg problem added another level of apprehension.

Okay let's do it. That first step was the crucial step of the run. All I wanted was a chance. *Please don't drop me in my tracks.* It didn't. They were three very stiff but pain-free steps. I was reminded of Jim Carrey's character in *Dumb and Dumber.* "So you're saying there's a chance!"

Steven Cannon

Green Bay would be the overnight for Day Thirteen. Our host, the Van Sistine family, was the family of my great friend Paco from Denver. It was a destination we had looked forward to from the start. Jarred and I knew that real beds, home-cooked food, and TLC awaited.

After dressing and eating, I shut the RV door behind me and told Jarred I'd see him a couple miles down the road. It was the plan to walk the first two miles and hope that the right leg would warm to the task.

I had formed a real bond with the lake. She had cooled me each day so I could eat real food. Her frigid waters had provided my ice bath at the end of every day. I truly believed she was there for me. I respected her and frequently recalled the famous saying about Everest: "You don't climb Mt. Everest... Mt. Everest lets you climb her." I considered myself a guest of the lake and asked her permission to run around her, giving her the props she deserved and asking her help at every turn. I had prayed to her the night before as I sat in her waters with a leg that would barely hold me. I had asked her to heal me and truly believed she could and would.

Each painless step that morning gave me just a little more confidence. Maybe it had just been a bad dream last night and not any kind of foreshadowing. A mile or so into the walk I was feeling much more confident. If need be, I would walk every damn mile that day and be grateful I could.

The shooting pain of the night before was gone. I contemplated whether to attempt a jog. Maybe it would be best to just walk it out, a sort of day off. That probably would have been a wise course of action, a safe play. I don't believe life is meant to be a safe play. I knew I could walk, and if the legs wouldn't let me run, I could fall back on the walk.

So, I started to run. It was not a pace that would win any races, but I was not here to win a race. I was here to raise money for those who choose to take one more step into uncertainty everyday. They believe that if they keep moving forward, refusing to give in, they will emerge better from the journey. I agreed and kept moving forward until I reached my destination.

Paco's folks were waiting on the front steps when we rolled up to their place. It felt so good to be there. They welcomed us with big smiles and kind words. We immediately felt like family. Momma Van Sistine (Sandi) was amazing. She took over: showers, laundry, drinks, and a nap for me. She didn't miss a beat. I swear, I was cleaned up, watered, fed, and down for a nap in ten minutes. I awoke later to a full grill out on the back porch. You would have thought Jarred had known these kind people forever the way they were getting along. The drinks were flowing, and grilled seafood and veggies were ready to be served. Papa Van Sistine (Gary) was a grill master! It was one of our favorite evenings of the entire run.

As I laid my head on the pillow that night in Green Bay, I again reflected on the many people in the cancer fight whom I had been so fortunate to meet the past years. I had learned so many lessons from them. They had showed me the power of hope and belief. Tomorrow I would take another step into uncertainty just like they had taught me.

Day 14

Does Monday morning suck?

I woke each day when my body was ready, usually between 7 a.m. and 8 a.m., with only one goal. I wanted to make it to the toilet and do so without anything in my legs or feet failing. That was it. Then I would attempt to choke down breakfast. When did eggs and bacon become so distasteful? The smell of food cooking in the morning activated my gag reflex almost instantly. In my "normal" life, breakfast was my favorite meal. This was not normal, however. There were times I felt like one of those guys in the hotdog-eating contests. I'd stuff as much as possible in my mouth, chew it, attempting not to taste it, try to wash it down, and repeat. I never had to actually use the pinch-the-nose trick our parents had taught us, but the thought did occur to me during many morning meals.

Back home, it had seemed that weather forecasters never batted much better than .500. They were on a real hitting streak now! Day One forecast...hottest ever. Yep. Day Two, slightly less hot. Yep.

71

FORTY DAYS

Day Three, hot with a high probability of extended hotness. Yep. Yep. Yep. "Come On!" I thought. "How about a swing and a miss?"

Nope. I stepped out the door and quickly realized that the weather forecasters were still in the groove. It was just a bit before 9 a.m., and it was....you guessed it...*hot*. It didn't feel like work though. It was not a job to be done or a clock to be punched. There was no Sunday-evening-before-the-work-week dread feeling to it. There was a joy, a passion, a purpose. Even during the most challenging of times, the answers to the questions "Where would you rather be? What would you rather be doing?" were always the same. "Nowhere. Nothing."

Day Fourteen seemed possible. Everything seemed possible.

I used to wonder what made some people super successful while others languished. Was it talent? Was it work ethic? Was there a certain thread running through the fabric of success? I think it is important to emphasize that my idea of success and "the real world's" definition of success differ. We live in a very materialistic society. *He who has the most toys wins.* Many who accumulate the most toys speak of something missing. It is this something that I believe should be one's guide to success. You can call it passion, purpose, or a calling. It is as much a feeling as it is anything else. A wise person once said, "Do what you would do for free and then find a way to get paid for it." The message is this: Follow your heart in all things, and success is the only possible outcome. This is not to say that effort is not involved or that there are never setbacks; of course there are. The common thread running through all super success stories is a love for what you do. It is the fuel. There is never the dread of Monday morning work. In fact there is no such thing as work. Each day brings new excitement and the chance to cre-

Steven Cannon

ate. There is no grind, no punching the clock. You are in the flow, and all parts of your life reflect it. Follow your heart. The universe supports everyone who does so unequivocally. No exceptions. The leap may scare the hell out of you, but no one who has taken it has ever regretted it.

Day 15

The power of WE

Wow! How the hell have we made it four hundred miles?

It was always "we," never "I." I'm not sure how far I could go on my own. I'm not sure it is possible to go anywhere meaningful alone. I remember my niece texting me at the end of the fourth day: "Dude, you just ran to Milwaukee!!" Now we were headed towards Michigan, our third state. I began to think about all those who had gotten me to this point. I was in no real hurry to make the three-step pilgrimage to the toilet, so I was more than content to ponder such things laying in bed.

There were the obvious folks, Jarred being number one. It was unfathomable to me how he does it. Drive a mile or two, stop, wait, wait, wait, repeat. Wash water bottles, wait, wait, wait, get food ready, wait, wait, wait. Hour after hour, day after day. There are few real certainties, but this I was sure of: I would not have made it 400 miles without him. His dedication was beyond remarkable. Then there was my coach, Ray Zahab, who donated his time to train me, all while planning his own expeditions and running his incredible organization, www.impossible2possible.com. My great friend, Steve Falck got us our RV. Many businesses made donations which helped with food, fuel, clothes, and more. Hundreds of people donated money to Livestrong and sent messages that were posted on the walls of the RV.

We also put pictures up throughout the vehicle. There was a picture of my friend Darin Ferguson. I remembered back to a time spent in the pool together, after he had been diagnosed with leukemia. His lungs were so wrecked from chemo, swimming a single length of the pool left him gasping for air. He would work to catch his breath and go again...and again...and again. He's now a cancer survivor, a big time fundraiser for Leukemia & Lymphoma Society, and a two time finisher of the Ironman triathlon!

There was a picture of a beautiful little boy named Eli Horn. Cancer took him from us one month before his eighth birthday. His father, Aaron, shared his story with us:

Eli was three and a half years old when he was diagnosed with a rare childhood cancer called neuroblastoma. When it was discovered, the tumor (which originates in one of the adrenal glands) had already expanded up into his chest, around his aorta and renal arteries to the kidneys, and down into his pelvis. We lived in Ames, Iowa at the time, and Eli was treated at the University of Iowa Hospitals for 30 days before our family moved to the largest Ronald McDonald House in the world in New York City so he could get treated at Memorial Sloan Kettering Cancer Center in Manhattan. MSKCC has been doing research on Neuroblastoma for decades and was, at that time, the only place in the world that offered 3F8 antibody treatment. The 3F8 antibody treatment worked in clearing Eli of the Neuroblastoma, but all of the chemo and radiation ended up causing secondary cancer (AML), and Eli passed away just before his eighth birthday on January 18th, 2012 during a stem cell transplant.

Like most younger kids fighting cancer, Eli didn't feel sorry for himself or ever consider the option of not fighting his disease. He went bravely into treatment and did what he had to do, no matter how painful. While 3F8 is very effective for some kids, it also brings excruciating pain because the drug not only highlights the neuroblastoma cells so that the white blood cells will attack them, but it also highlights nerve endings, so the white blood cells are also causing extreme pain. Eli would walk into the hospital in the morning, go through very painful treatment, go back to the Ronald McDonald House to recover and play, then jump right back onto the hospital bed the next day for more treatment. He had the same approach to his multiple surgeries, vomit inducing and hair destroying chemo, scary scans in big machines, copious amounts of medicine, and daily pokes and vital checks. He just wanted to get it over with so he could go back to being a normal kid and playing with his other friends and little brother Isaiah. Only once did Eli ask why God let him get cancer, but he was sure that God allowed it to happen because he was strong enough to handle it. He knew that God would use the situation to impact lives, and he certainly did. Throughout Eli's journey, thousands of people from around the world read Eli's blog (www.elihorn.com) and felt a strong connection to a little boy they had never met. Years after his passing, people are still impacted by the life of a brave little boy that taught them not to sweat the small stuff and remember what was truly important in life.

In 2009, I became involved with a few other families in Iowa that wanted to raise money for research and family support programs. We started selling t-shirts that simply said "BEAT CANCER" on the front. They had great success, so in 2012 we became an official 501(c)3 nonprofit called Beat Cancer Today, Inc. Eli loved wearing his Beat Cancer shirts around Iowa and New York City. Beat Cancer Today (www.beatcancertoday.org) still sells BEAT CANCER apparel in various colors for schools and businesses and donates the money raised to three different organizations. The University of Iowa Dance Marathon is one of the largest student run philanthropies in the United States. They offer financial aid and support programs for families being treated at the U of I for childhood cancer. Children's Cancer Connection is another group that Beat Cancer supports, and they also offer family and patient support programs, as well as summer camps for oncology patients and their siblings to attend free of charge. The Children's Oncology Group is a national research organization dedicated solely to childhood cancer research, as the National Cancer Institute only gives around 4% of its research budget to childhood cancer research.

When a child passes away, a parent's greatest fear is that their child will be forgotten. The greatest gift someone can give a grieving parent is to talk about their child and the impact they had on their life. People often fear that they'll be reminding the parent of what they lost, but it is something they think about everyday, so it is far better to let them know that they miss the child as well and that they think about them often. Eli truly impacted more lives in his almost eight years on earth than many people do in a lifetime.

FORTY DAYS

I was certainly one of those many lives Eli impacted.

–Aaron Horn
http://about.me/aaronhorn
http://www.elihorn.com
http://www.beatcancertoday.org

There was a picture of a beautiful young lady in a "f*ck cancer" t-shirt. Her name was Jaime De Hayes. Her sister Jenna shared the following:

J'aime: French for like, love, fancy, cherish, engage, and care—a beautiful word and my sister's name. The meaning of J'aime is why my parents decided to name my sister Jaime. Anyone who was familiar with Jaime would describe her using this same definition. My grandpa Jarvis once said to my mom when Jaime was just a little girl that he knew that she was special, that there was just something really extraordinary about her, but he wasn't sure why just yet. He was a wise man and was exactly right about Jaime being special. She was an angel on earth from the moment she was born to the day god decided her good work was complete. She is now my family's guardian angel. She will always be the most special person in my heart, my number one sister, my best friend, hero, and inspiration. She is my sister angel.

Even though she was named after that beautiful French word, most people would say that there really are no exact words or ways to describe her inner and outer beauty. That is just how extraordinary she was. It's like trying to describe heaven. She had this contagious laugh that made everyone smile, her love for kids was magical, and her passion for life was so strong. She was so positive all the time, always wanting to help others with their problems and struggles. I will never forget when she told me about when she went to the store, and at the check-out behind her was a woman counting her change. It was clear that the woman didn't have enough money for what she was buying so Jaime gave the cashier money to pay for the rest of the woman's bill. She is an example of what everyone strives to be. She never had to think twice about doing things like this- it just came naturally.

At the young age of 29 Jaime got terrifying news that she had stage three colorectal cancer. This is not normal news at 29. It was devastating, a shock to everyone. There were so many questions around how this could be. As physically and emotionally difficult this experience was for her she surprised so many people with her perseverance and determination. She came up with the slogan, "Beauty Beats Cancer." BBC (for short) kept her spirits high and fueled her bravery. To her there were no decision to make, she was determined to fight. She wasn't going to let the disease control her. She was going to control it. From then on we were all in this together. My family was strong, but we got stronger. As sisters we were the four musketeers, Jackie, Jaime, Jill, and me (Jenna). What's special about our relationship is that we're also best friends. We were always committed to getting Jaime through her battle no matter what it took. We were going to win.

Through a lot of intense chemotherapy treatments and radiation, she continued to go to work and do everyday things because she knew if she started to feel bad for herself or stopped doing her everyday routine it would affect her attitude. She quickly became not only an inspiration to me but also a hero to everyone else around her. She went through a surgery to remove the cancer, but it didn't go as planned. The surgery resulted in her requiring colostomy bag. The cancer has attacked too much of her colon, and doctors couldn't save any of her large intestine. As anyone can imagine this was devastating news to a young beautiful woman. It was an extremely hard change to get accustomed to. She had so many questions, concerns, and worries. One minute she had normal working organs, and the next she woke up to a completely changed life. Jaime was strong-minded, not allowing this to change her positive outlook. She was going to live through it, just another step in getting rid of the disease. With everyone's support and her strong-willed personality, she got back to her old self, nicknaming her colostomy bag and all. She would even make jokes about it-not allowing it to define her. She was still Jaime.

"Never blame a day in your life. Always remember a good day gives you happiness, and a bad day gives you experience"-Jaime

My family put on a Beauty Beats Cancer fundraiser for her shortly after the diagnosis. This was when Beauty Beats Cancer really started to become more than just a slogan. It was now a part of our lives. We made Blue Beauty Beats Cancer bracelets and T-shirts which help raise money for her treatments. Soon everyone around town and friends states away wanted to order them. The night of her fundraiser was more than magical. Not only did we raise a great amount of money and raise awareness, but Jaime also reconnected with her high school sweetheart, Tom. It was like no time had passed. Tom had never stopped loving Jaime from the day they started dating in high school. I had known him since I was 10 years old, and he was already seemingly a brother to me. Their college careers had separated them until that night. It is a true love story, reminiscent of a fairy tale. He promised her he would never leave her side again, and he told her he was going to take care of her, that they would beat this together. He was determined from then on on that he would get rid of her cancer. She had found the one that wanted her for who she was and what she was going through was nothing compared to the amount of love he had for her. He proposed to her a year later.

On Jaime and Tom's wedding day Jaime was in remission. She was still getting chemo every couple of weeks, and then she would get scans, but the scans were looking stable, and she was feeling the best she had felt in a while. That day she looked like an angel on earth. There is no doubt in my mind that God was there protecting her and making sure she was feeling her best. This was her fairy tale come true, and that day and night was the happiest my family has ever seen her. I thank God every day that she was able to have that special day with no reminders of her disease- to us she was cancer free.

She was continuing her "maintenance" treatments and was living her life with more passion and love than before. She was so thankful for getting to where she was, being married to Tom, and the most thankful for her life and the people that have stayed by her side.

"Dear Lord, thank you for all you have done for me and given me. I ask that you would watch over me and my loved ones. That you would cover us with your protection. Let all who take refuge in you rejoice; let them ever sing for joy, and spread your protection over them, that those who love your name may exult in you. For you bless the righteous, O LORD; you cover him with favor as with a shield. Thank you Lord for hearing my prayer. In Jesus' Holy name, AMEN!" -Jaime

FORTY DAYS

This is one of many prayers that she wrote on Facebook. To me these were words of an angel, it was so natural and second nature to her. She touched so many people with her inspirational words and the things that she did.

A few weeks later she was starting to feel tightness in her chest and shortness of breath, and the doctors found that the colorectal cancer had metastasized to her lungs. This was the hardest news yet. Tom started to do more research on alternative medicine and was still determined that he would get her the miracle that she deserved. He never gave up hope, they were going to live a long life together. He was her saving grace, he made sure that she got to enjoy all the beautiful things in the world. He treated her like a queen because she deserved it. There are not enough words to describe his passion and infinite love for her- as far as Jaime was concerned he was giving her a miracle, and he didn't even know it.

"I am blessed with a life not many could handle... thank you god for giving me the strength, courage and most perfect husband to guide me through. God bless EVERYONE!"-Jaime

She was so thankful all the way to the end. She continued to stay stronger than anyone I knew without cancer. She wouldn't surrender, and Tom wouldn't either. She did breathing treatments and chemo and had to be on oxygen most of the time during the day. Her treatments were stabilizing the cancer in her lungs which was music to our ears. It was good news to her and my family that it was not spreading, and some of the tumors were actually getting smaller. This was something to be celebrated. Our prayers, positivity, love and faith were making a difference.

"Scan results...stable in both lungs, no change BUT.... improved in left lung! BBC- I'm going to beat this sun of a monster!!!"-Jaime

People that didn't even know Jaime started to message me, my

Steven Cannon

family, and Jaime to say how her perseverance and bravery have really touched them. She helped people realize why everyday was so special. She made people realize that life is short and to enjoy every day, treat people the way you would want to be treated, to not complain if something doesn't turn out the way was expected, and that life is precious. These are things that people in this world know they should live by, but many get caught up in the wrong motivations. She touched people's lives in a way that was miraculous. Hundreds and thousands of miles away from her were people that didn't know her but knew someone in our family, and they would tell us how she changed their life in some positive way. She would write on Facebook so many great lessons about life.

"I don't believe you have to be better than everyone else... I believe you have to be better than you ever thought you could ever be..."

She received this anonymous message one day, and we still do not know who sent it.

Hey there, I have always loved you, please don't focus on who I am, but who you are and who you have become. I love you, I always have, I always will. Not in a romantic way! I wanted you to have this little poem I wrote for you when I heard in March. I just deal with stuff differently than most people, it does not mean I was not with you all the way...keep it up girl, you rock... Isn't it great when you find out who's got your back now? I adore you and always will. Sorry to be mysterious, I just keep stuff within, yet I hope you love my thoughts of you, and this little poem...

FORTY DAYS
SONG BIRDS OF BEAUTY

We hear the birds sing and often wonder why, then all at once darkness fills their sky.

But now the birds sing louder than they ever did before, hearts are broken, strength is tested, pain is   at the door.

For the enemy is faceless, mindless, and does not play fair, with it comes worry, wonder, fear, and despair.

Memories flood back to our rights and our wrongs, we loved the soundtrack, we wrote all the songs.

We have many encores, rhymes, notes, and more words, to sing in the future, to the delight of the birds.

So here's to our next song, play it loud, play it clear. Though this ballad starts slowly, the lyrics are so dear.

It's about a hero and a guarantee for better days, the song is beautiful it's called Jaime DeHayes.

The last time I ever got to hear her voice again was over the phone. She always made me promise that we wouldn't talk about how she was feeling- she wanted to focus on other things. We would talk at least once a day just to say 'hi' and make each other laugh. The next thing I knew my family and I were in Arizona with her and Tom in the ICU. She had to be put on a respirator that would breathe for her for the rest of her time. They stopped her treatment because the cancer had taken over her lungs, there were no surgeries or treatments to make it better, just our love, and hope. Tom was still determined to get her that miracle. He would bring her different alternative medicines, and vitamins that he researched and believed would give her the miracle; he was not letting this miracle pass her by. She made the nurses help her walk the halls with machines alongside of her. She still wasn't going to let the cancer define her. She would not give in to the battle that cancer gave her.

Jaime had already received her miracle. I am confident that she knew this from the moment she saw Tom again the night of her fundraiser. My mom gave birth to a miracle named J'aime, and she was everything this word means and more- she is the definition of like; love; fancy, cherish, engage, and care. She was born for a reason, and that reason was to teach everyone a lesson about life. To give them hope, to keep fighting for what they believe in, to love everyone for who they are, to help others even when they don't ask for it, to believe in themselves, to live everyday of their lives with a smile and to laugh often.

"I believe in miracles, I believe in fate, I believe that I can make a difference, and I have faith that everything that's happened has made me who I am today."-Jaime

She made sure to teach this lesson to her three musketeer sisters. She made sure that we learned the most important things in life so that we could all carry on this lesson. On May 9th 2012, Jaime's good work on earth was finished, and from then on it has been the musketeers' job to keep her spirit alive through stories like this, making sure people remember what life is all about. I know I will never be as good of a person as she was, but I sure hope to be at least half as good one day. We are keeping her alive not only by having these opportunities to write about her but also by being part of Colon Cancer Foundations, by raising awareness and even by starting a foundation for her named Beauty Beats Cancer.

I leave you with one of Jaime's last prayers, one that makes me believe that she knew she was here on earth for a reason, and once she knew she was sick she knew that she could make a difference.

FORTY DAYS

She is my *sauveur*, my best friend, my hero, and my inspiration. Without her I wouldn't be where I am today. She truly is my sister angel.

"Dear LORD, I thank you for giving your life on the cross for me. I place my whole being into your hands. I humbly ask you to fill me with your Holy Spirit, to stay with me always, to help and guide me. LORD, help me to be open, to listen and follow where Your Spirit guides me. I ask this in Jesus' name, AMEN."-Jaime"

These incredible stories always buoyed me. Their journey, their courage, teach us that we can always dig deeper, go farther. They were my constant reminders to never give up. Every day, without fail, I'd get text messages from my mom. In addition, there were many, many messages every hour on Facebook, Twitter, email, etc. This morning was the first time I had really looked at them in totality. The support was seemingly endless and incredibly empowering. It has been said that nothing worth doing is worth doing alone. I believe I would amend that to say nothing worth doing is *possible* doing alone. There was no way to know how far the tentacles of this run stretched out or how many people it was touching. It was evident to me at that moment that I had an almost endless reserve of people who were pulling for me, both in the physical realm and beyond. It was a special moment laying there, feeling so loved and supported. The day had started with a somewhat groggy question: "How the hell have we made it four hundred miles?" The answer filled me with the strength of ten men. I chuckled thinking of the Grinch and "his heart growing two sizes that day, they say."

Time to get your ass moving! I thought. And with that I was out of bed, ready to take that always necessary first step.

Day 16

The gift of cancer

What is it like to feel the love and support of so many every day? Is it possible you can get the "gift" of cancer without having to endure the pain and sickness? I was now able to answer these questions. Words can not encompass all that this is. Imagine the feeling of your best hug *ever*. Take just a moment, and go to that place and soak it in. Do you remember the first time your parents were really proud of you, or gave you that last little push that got you down the road without training wheels for the first time? Imagine a great big Saint Bernard just bowling you over and drenching you with two or three big dog kisses. It is all of this and more. I have heard many speak of the "gift" of cancer. They speak of how their life is now filled with so much more feeling, love, and gratitude because they have had to face their mortality and take stock of where they are and what is truly important in this life.

They have shared the "gift" with me through the stories of their

FORTY DAYS

journeys. I have seen their strength and passion for life. I hope I am repaying that gift through my efforts to raise money for those who are battling this disease. I certainly will always be on the "owe" side of the ledger. Take a few deep breaths, and take in the following messages that fueled our run around Lake Michigan. It is my hope that you too may find benefit or motivation from them.

—My son died of a brain tumor on June 24, 1996 at the age of 3 years, 7 months, 19 days. He fought an innocent, yet courageous battle for 2 years, 9 months. It still hurts. But God sustains my family through it all. Thank you

—Dude, We are so proud of you and everything you are doing! We know you can do it, and please know, we will be with you every step of the way!! Run, Forest, Run!! Your Sister

—I have just begun running, actually more of a jogger. You are an inspiration. Keep Living Strong!

—What a wonderful and challenging event you are doing. Your efforts have undoubtedly opened more eyes.

—Love hearing about the wonderful people who are running with you and keeping you going. They've got to be a great inspiration. Keep going baby. We are with you. Mom

—HEY FUNCLE!!! We love you so much and keep on pushin! Good Luck Man, Love your favorite nieces and nephew

—Hey Steve, the Livestrong family is cheering you on, your commitment to help others inspires us all!!!!!! RUN STRONG/LIVESTRONG! The Greater Des Moines Area Livestrong Chapter

—We know you can do it Steve!!!! Know that we are thinking of you!

—I am so moved and inspired by what you are doing. As I sit here in my sticky, but comfortable house, I cannot even fathom being in this heat like you are! You're the best, hang in there!!!

Steven Cannon

—Steve, keep pushin brother! I just wanted to say that right now, more than ever, I am damn proud to call you my friend, my mentor, and my hero. thats right canjo- you are my hero. I'm proud of you my man. Now get out there in the morning and DO WORK!

—Good luck on your run my Brother! We're rooting for you from Salt Lake City.

—Go Duder go! im sending some beautiful rocky mountain 80 degree weather your way..

—cheers brutha!

—Steve, I had so much fun running with you! It was such a great experience and changed my views on a lot of things! You are such a great influence and inspiration to everyone, including me. You are also a wonderful role model and I admire that. That 21 miles taught me a lot and I won't forget it!! It was super super hot on the road and extremely hilly but we made it and thats all that counts. =))

—I was pleasantly surprised to pass you last night. I was so excited and can even say I felt a great sense of pride knowing that I have chosen to become involved with people like you who are raising funds for such a worthy cause (it also motivated me to get re-energized and keep working on my own LAF fundraising for RAGBRAI).

—Good morning Steve, the weather has tried, but failed to stop you, Have another strong and safe day, your journey is helping many!

—Thank you Soooooooo Much to all the wonderful people who are supporting Steve and running with him. He's MY Hero. Steve's Mom

—It was great to see you yesterday. Just let all of the people you have met on this incredible journey, all of the stories you have heard and all of the lives you have touched carry you. You are one amazing guy and we are all extremely proud of you. Talk to you soon.

—Steve, you are such an inspiration to me. I love you so much and I *hope that the wind is at your back during these last couple days. Mom already said it, and I hate to be redundant, but it's true. You're our hero.*

—In 2011, I lost my godmother to brain tumor after an 18 month struggle, and only a two weeks later my mom was diagnosed with terminal cancer. She did not even get a chance to fight and was gone within 3 weeks…I want to help fighting this most unpredictable and powerful beast.

—I am very inspired and will be there to run for my sister Jaime (30yrs old) who is suffering but fighting against colon/rectal cancer which has now attacked her lungs. she is a fighter and doesn't care what the dr.s say..she is a fighter and wont give up. I will be joining to run for her and to fight for her and to give all my strength to her. Thank you Steve (Jaime lost her fight just weeks before the run around Lake Michigan)

—Steve my old friend….I have seen the tragedy of cancer unfold in my life with many of my closest friends the past few years. All my best wishes.

—As if on eagle's wings, soar brother—

—Very inspiring! I would love to run with you! Good for you for taking the initiative! Screw you cancer…you can't take this smile from my face!

—My 46 year old sister in law is currently battling small cell carcinoma in her brain, lungs, liver and spine. I ran for her last year and it was very satisfying using my health to promote a cure for hers! Keep Running! God bless you! Kick cancer's butt!

—Very Inspiring, great work. Together we can beat the cancer. I cannot tell how much I love to join you but physical location makes it difficult. Lots of wishes from India.

Steven Cannon

—Wow! you are a true inspiration. My dad was diagnosed with stage 4 Colon cancer in Aug 2011. His doctor estimated him to live about 6 months. It has now been about 9 months and he's still living strong. I would love to run with you! Best of luck!

—How very humbling to read that Steve ran in the very conditions that forced the race organizers to cancel the Madison Marathon! And then woke up to do it all again for the next 39 days.

—Ran my half in highland park yesterday and it was brutally hot!! Thought of you every step of the way and enlightened some others about your journey. Can't believe you're in Michigan already!!! Keep on Truckin!!

—Remember... "The woods are lovely, dark and deep, but I have promises to keep, and miles to go before I sleep. And miles to go before I sleep!"

—Today you run for Uncle Mike who was diagnosed with Stomach Cancer. Love you. Mom

—Steve Cannon, dig deep today. Be present to the moment. You are changing your life and the lives of others with every step. Don't you kid yourself, you know this is making a difference. Keep it together, keep positive, you can do anything when you know there is an end, you may not see it right now, but it is coming and that experience will be amazing! Sending strength and love your way my friend!!!

—Steve, We are all cheering you on here in Des Moines, buddy! I met you while riding Survivor Cross last fall…what an event that was. But not nearly as incredible as the event you are tackling now in the name of cancer. I just wanted to say thanks. For friends past, for my uncle who died a few years back, and especially for my father who is in hospice suffering through the very last stages of cancer now…thank you for taking up this fight, and for inspiring us to do the same. Your efforts *and your pain are not going unnoticed. Press on, my friend. Mike*

—I just read about your run in the Traverse City paper this morning. I ran the Chicago Marathon as part of Team Livestrong and am constantly amazed by the people who are a part of this wonderful Foundation. I would love to join you on part of your run in the Traverse City area tomorrow if possible! You truly are an inspiration!

—Was sitting here in Austin talking to my mom in DSM. She said in passing, "there's some guy that's going to run like 40 marathons in 40 days for the Livestrong Foundation" while she was reading the Des Moines Register. I said, "holy crap he's really doing it!!!"

—Steve, Although I wanted to be there to celebrate you, and what you have achieved for thousands of people, please know that all of your family here is so proud of you and what you have accomplished. I know Uncle Mike was with you, and would've been the first to say "Hell of a job nephew". God bless – Aunt Mary

—Love all the stories about how people seem to show up right when you need 'em Steve! I've been thinking of you every day in this ungodly heat... I truly don't know how you manage it! Stay strong... one foot in front of the other... you are so so close!

—Steve, reading this post and seeing my grandma's name mentioned is so heartwarming. I never got to meet her as she was taken by cancer shortly before I was born and I have always wished I would have gotten the chance to meet her. Having pictures of Grandma Dewey is such a blessing but there is still the awful void of missing the times I could have spent with her. What you are doing is so amazing and I send my prayers and positive energy your way

—This led to a whole new level of inspiration for me. I think you've started a revolution amongst us. Congrats, Steve – you've done it again!

Day 17

Can you see YOU?

"WHADDAYAMEAN???"

That response, combined with a glazed over look on the face of the person asking, is the true litmus test of any adventure. A decade earlier I had decided to strike out on a two-month bike tour from Iowa and head west. There was only one certain destination. That was the starting line for the Deadwood Mickelson trail marathon in South Dakota. It was 600 miles away, and I had twelve days to get there. A couple days prior to arriving in Deadwood, after pulling into a convenience store somewhere in eastern South Dakota, it happened. The fully loaded bike always invited questions. "Where you riding from?" the cashier asked. "Des Moines, Iowa, headed to Deadwood", I replied. The eyes began to glaze, followed by an accompanying blank stare. A few quiet moments ensued as her mind raced to compute. Unable to do so, all she had left was to reply,

FORTY DAYS

"WHADDAYAMEAN???" Adventure litmus test passed. It was the first of what would become many such stories.

The further north the run took us, the less populated the area became. Seldom on straight roads, we had no way to know if any sign of civilization waited around the next bend. Probably not. The RV would not be too far ahead, the inner GPS informed me. It seemed this stretch had been more than the usual two-mile max. Rounding the bend in the road, the convenience-looking mart ahead explained why. Jarred had probably decided that going just a bit further and stopping there made sense, which of course it did. It turned out to be just a few tenths of a mile longer than two miles. I was pretty pleased with how well my mental Garmin was working. Instantly my mind delighted, *Chocolate milk!* We had recently exhausted our supply. It sounded so good. The lady behind the counter was super-friendly, and it became obvious from all the local knowledge she was laying on us that she was from the area. Noticing the RV outside she inquired, "What you fellas up to?" It was my favorite question, and I stood quietly waiting to see how this would play out. Jarred chimed right in. "We are on a run to raise money for cancer." I thought to myself, "Well played Jarred: just enough, but not too much info." This would certainly bait the hook. Unable to resist, she followed up with, "Oh, that's nice, where you running from?" Jarred held his response just for a moment for effect and let her have it. One word, "Chicago." The glazing of the eyes, the delay in the response, the face losing expression. Meltdown complete, she stuttered, "WHADDAYAMEAN???"

Back in the RV, we shared a big laugh, as I savored the delicious chocolate moo juice. We had a lot of fun imagining her sharing our story with future customers.

Steven Cannon

A little early in the day to be hitting the bottle, don't ya think?
You mean they were driving *from Chicago, don't you??*
Ha ha. Ran here from Chicago...Good one!

Armed with enough of these imagined conversations and enough chocolate milk, a guy could run for quite some time. Miles later, the quietness of the road struck me. I realized what a contrast it was to the norm. These *aha* moments were becoming much more frequent. Our world is full of so much noise. There is increasingly less and less time to just be quiet. Imagine just a few hours with no email, no TV, no Internet. What would that be like for you? I can tell you that eventually your mind will revolt. It has become so used to the constant input that, given a few hours of pure quiet, it begins to starve. Meanwhile, with each passing hour, the soul drinks in the silence and grows stronger. If you can hold on long enough, you will slowly notice the waves of the mind turn to ripples, and the ripples eventually give way to a total calm. It is in this calm that you can look and see the reflection of the real you.

I knew that eventually I would run to that place during this journey around Lake Michigan. Certainly I was running to raise money for those in the cancer fight, but I was also on a new, deeper journey of self discovery. I had enjoyed the excitement of those early days and endured the physical and mental tantrums. Now, with the day's running behind me, I sat looking out over Lake Michigan in a park that I most likely will never visit again. I was overcome by the sense of things. A sense of all things. A sense that comes from running out of one's mind. The noise had stopped. It was gone. The mind had become exactly like the giant

FORTY DAYS

Lake Michigan on a perfectly calm day. There were no waves, no ripples...just complete stillness. I had accessed that place of everything and nothing.

It was the place that I had caught a glimpse of when I was eleven years old, running home from school. That day, over thirty years ago, I had but scratched the surface. It only lasted for a few minutes, and as a youngster I could barely grasp the sense of it. There was a rhythm and an ease that slowly fell over me as I ran home that day. The pounding of my heart slowly began to quiet, and the sound of my feet hitting the sidewalk began to drift away. I was entering the flow of things but had no real concept of it. Running would not play any type of role in my life until decades later. Not until attempting to run across Iowa at forty-four years old did I ever even think about it. It was on that cross-state run that I had first delved much further into that space, spending hours and eventually days totally out of my mind.

Sitting on Lake Michigan's shores, I felt that a cold soak, hot shower, and dinner could wait. It felt right to try to put the moment into words. So I wrote:

As I sit here overlooking this incredible lake, I am reminded of what a blessed life I lead and have lived. I am sitting on a soft dirt trail covered in pine needles overlooking the water, and not a soul on this earth knows my location. I am known only to the gull that sings in the distance. I listen to what the wind has to say. The doe and her fawn that I ran by moments ago are somewhere near, closer than I probably know. I hope they all sense that I am their friend. I am a grateful visitor to this place they call home, and it is here that I sense my connection to everything. Namaste.

Day 18

Ode to Jarred

My mind went back to my training for the Iowa run. The smell of freshly roasted coffee filled the air. I am no coffee drinker, but is there anyone that doesn't enjoy that smell? I had stopped into the neighborhood roaster for a cup of morning tea. It was a great way to start the day and to warm the body from the inside out.

There was still a massive amount of planning to be done. At the top of the list was a support vehicle. A support vehicle, once found, would be of little use if there was no one to drive it. The first five days of the run were covered. I still needed to find someone to handle driving duties for the last six days of the adventure.

I'm a firm believer that the universe will provide in all endeavors. "Build it, and they will come." The universe was about to prove this true once again.

Jarred Harkin was a guy I had met years earlier on a bike ride called RAGBRAI, the (Des Moines) Register's Annual Great Bicy-

FORTY DAYS

cle Ride Across Iowa. He was a gentle giant of a guy with a good sense of humor. From time to time we'd run into each other at Friedrich's, a local coffee shop. Today the universe made sure we did that again. There was no way to foresee what that meeting would grow into—a relationship that transcends friendship.

We shot the bull for a few minutes, catching up on this and that. Eventually, we got around to what I was up to, and I said, "Hey, what are you doing in late June? I've got this little run I'm planning and could sure use a good man."

Jarred spends his professional life as a contractor. If it can be imagined, then he can build it. The dude has a work ethic that is hard to describe. As I started to share with him the plans to run across Iowa, it seemed as though he might be interested. It had been years since his last vacation, and after chatting for a short time more, he agreed to take the driving duties for the final six days of the run. Thank you, universe!

There was no way of knowing then what I know now. Truth be told, I would have let anyone drive that support vehicle. I couldn't do the run without it. If you had a license and could keep it out of the ditch, you were eligible. Hell, I don't think I would have even cared about the license. But with Jarred, I got so much more, and not just on that first run across Iowa.

For the Lake Michigan run, the goal was to get around Lake Michigan, 1,037 miles in forty days. People often asked, "How the hell did you do that?!" To which there are many different answers; "I just did," "One step at a time," and "I'm not exactly sure" are a few of them. The question for which I have no answer is, *How the hell did Jarred do it?* As I ran along the shoreline of *Mom* that day, I thought again about all he had done for me.

The early days of the run had been brutal. It was incredibly hot.

Steven Cannon

Food was not inviting, and my mind was staging its own revolts throughout the day. Yet, each morning without fail, Jarred had been up and at 'em in the kitchen. Day Four was a particularly tough day. I'd started later than normal, I couldn't eat, we stopped for interviews in Milwaukee, I took a much longer than expected nap, and I found myself with ten miles or so left as the sun went down. It ended up being almost midnight when we finished that day. While I ran, Jarred would drive one mile, wait. Drive two miles, wait. Mix new drinks to swap out. Make lunch for Steve. Cut up fruit because that's all he can eat right now. Drive one mile, wait. Sit and wait while Steve takes a nap. Do the dishes. Drive two miles, wait. Get out fresh socks and a change of shoes.

As I got out of my clothes that night, showered, and started my recovery for the next day, Jarred began dinner. He broke out all his cooking gear and got to work. He is an incredible cook and takes great pride in his craft. A double-burner stove with propane tanks provided him the makeshift kitchen he needed to prepare a fantastic homemade sauce spread over chicken pasta for dinner.

It was all I could do to stay awake after the hot shower. I remember nearly falling asleep in my food. Jarred kept me talking to ensure his meal didn't become a chicken pasta facial. He refilled my chocolate milk and sent me off to bed. My day was done. His still had an hour or more to go. It was already well past midnight. I remember hearing the occasional clank of pots and pans as I drifted off to sleep.

My thoughts were interrupted as I came back to the here-and-now and noticed the RV waiting for me just ahead. It was always a welcome sight. It meant I had just completed another mile or two. More than that, it meant I would see my friend again. How far we

FORTY DAYS

had come together since that fateful meeting in the coffee shop. I couldn't have done it without him and still have no idea how he did it. Day Eighteen was nearly done.

Day 19

Get out there!

Today was a day to reminisce.

"I was pretty sure you'd end up being just some punk kid from the city, never amounting to much," my Uncle Bob shared with me when I was well into my forties. We used to head up to Fort Dodge quite a bit when I was young. We always had a good time. Most of my mom's family was there, and they were all half crazy, in a good way. Aunt Mary (my mom's sister) and Uncle Bob were fun folks. They had a son, Brian, about my age, and we got along really well. I can remember laughing a lot.

Uncle Bob made me curious about the things he did. I didn't understand much of what he did or why, but I was intrigued. As I look back now, certainly he lit a flicker of a flame that was searching for oxygen.

Every fall there would be a morning in Fort Dodge when we woke to commotion. I'd get out of bed to find Uncle Bob and Brian in the garage and a dead deer hanging from the garage rafters. My biggest question was probably, "Just how dang early did they get up this morning?" Followed by, "I sure am glad they didn't ask me to go." I find it funny that, many years later, hunting whitetail deer and learning the outdoors became a great passion for me. Another year, I can remember going into their basement to find a giant canoe under construction. Uncle Bob was building himself a boat. From scratch. It was beautiful. He was that kind of guy; hunter, craftsman, dog trainer, you name it, he could have done it had he put his mind to it.

I was excited when Uncle Bob invited me on a Boundary Waters adventure a few years later. To this day, I'm not sure why he invited the "punk kid". Maybe someone had invited him on a similar trip when he was young, and it changed his life for the better. It certainly changed mine.

Mom's only requirement for me to go had been that my grades were good. It had been some time since my report card had been much to look at. I had one thing in my favor: report cards would not be out until *after* the trip. I knew I was failing one class and, if lucky, a B and a few Cs would round out the rest of the card. I decided to commit to "Can't be sure, Mom, but probably all Bs and Cs." The "F" would be a deal breaker so I decided to take the punishment upon my return.

I'll never forget the feeling during the drive north towards Canada from Fort Dodge. I get the same feeling with every adventure still today—so alive and full of energy. It feels like I am honoring my time here on earth. We are not meant to sit in cubicles and punch time clocks day after day. There is no juice in that. We are here to live BIG exciting lives full of adventure. I am convinced that no one anywhere ever thought at the end of their life, "Wow, if I could have had just one more day in the cubicle!" When my time comes to leave this earth, and my life passes before my eyes, will it be a movie worth watching? I don't want to have to say, "Well it was alright...worth renting maybe, but I wouldn't pay full price to watch it." I'm planning on a "two thumbs up" rating!

The country around the Boundary Waters was so much bigger than anything I had ever seen. It was all so wild, forests and water everywhere you looked. It may as well have been the "Land of Ten Million Lakes" instead of ten thousand. The water was so crystal clear; I found a pair of sunglasses in six feet of water. Retrieving them required a breath-stealing dive into the lake. My eyes were being opened in new ways everyday. A seed was being planted. Rather, I should say, a seed was being watered. I don't think it's a stretch to say that trip, more than any other event in my childhood, led me to the life I lead now. *Thanks, Uncle Bob.*

Day 20

What running can be

Running has so much to offer beyond the physical. Those who judge their running success by time and distance miss a great opportunity. It is similar to judging the ocean only by what is visible from the shore. In both cases, just beyond the surface lies an endless resource for those who wish to explore.

Breathe in, breathe out, breathe in, breathe out...in...out. Running is my meditation. I said earlier that running was a vehicle to lose the false and gain the real. That vehicle lets me calm my mind and connect to everything that is real, both inside and out. I witness random thoughts as they pass by, many at first, but as I let them pass freely without attachment or judgment, they begin to slow and eventually just stop. Breathe in, out, in, out. Even the act of breathing changes. Everything becomes less of a *doing* and more of a *being.*

I was connecting more deeply with the *real* with each passing step, mile, and day. Each moment was unique and given its due. None more important than the next. In reality there is never a next, each moment just is. With the distractions of everyday life far behind me, I was more present than at any other time in my life.

My mind had quieted many days prior. It existed now only to alert me of any bodily malfunctions and to provide basic survival reminders: like when to drink, when to walk a bit, and when to eat. Mind really wasn't necessary anymore, and I had come to peace with that many days ago.

I was now exploring the depths of what running has to offer below the surface of time and distance. If people would run without a watch or GPS for just a week, they would be amazed at how much richer their jaunt would be. They would experience a much deeper connection to all that is outside of and within themselves. They would swim in the true joy of what running offers to all those who are searching.

The past ten days had been a bit of a blur. There was no longer a reason to know if it was Tuesday or Saturday. Things like days of the week had stopped being of any importance many, many miles ago. Time had lost its meaning.

In reality, no step was more important than the next or the one that preceded it. Yet I could not deny that the first step of the run was, and the last step would be, special. There were also to be a few special days. Today was to be one of them. Today I was running towards a milestone: the halfway point of the run, the point at which each step would then take me closer to where I had begun this journey instead of farther from it.

My calm was broken a bit as I noticed the RV in the distance. Soon the day would be done. My mind began to chatter random thoughts of excitement, praise, and all kinds of wahoo-ing. *Breathe in, breath out...in...out...in...* As I arrived at the RV, I was as present as I could be. I had run over 500 miles with both Jarred's support and the support of family, friends, and people I would never know. Tomorrow that first step would be one step closer to Navy Pier. I would run north no more.

Stay in the moment. It is a lesson learned in distance running. There were twenty days to go if I was to return to the exact place I'd taken the first step of this run. Many nights prior I had broken my mind, ignored its incessant cries to the point that it finally gave up. To spend even an instant contemplating the five hundred more miles ahead of me, the twenty more days to go, the next day, or even as little as the end of the current day would serve as the mind's wake-up call, and that was something I did not want to invite.

Day 21

Dance around the fire. Howl at the moon.

Michigan's Upper Peninsula, known to locals as the UP, is one of Mother Nature's true treasures. Many years ago, a group of us had traveled here for a thirty-six-hour adventure race. Adventure racing is a great way to experience a place. A day and a half of running, biking, rappelling, orienteering, and kayaking immerses you fully into a place. I remembered being quite groggy after forty hours of racing with no sleep, but the area had left an impression, and it was exciting to be back. In a world that continues to become more and more developed and crowded, there are fewer and fewer wild places left. The Upper Peninsula is still one of those mostly untouched places. It was rare even to see a car pass by.

The run had taken us over five hundred miles so far, the equivalent of twenty marathons since we had left Navy Pier. In some ways, it seemed like yesterday. Yet at times it seemed a lifetime ago. Each day provided its own unique beauty. That was the joy of this challenge. Lake Michigan was always there, just off my right shoulder. If that was the only thing I saw each day, it would be more than enough, but there was often more—so much more. The next few days we would run amongst the giant pines of the UP. "The land above the bridge" is an adventurer's utopia. The land mass takes up nearly a third of the state, yet boasts less than 3% of its population. It reminded me of the Yukon in many ways; the long harsh winters combined with very short days during those months kept the area nicely untouched by man. It was not unusual for 200 inches of snow to fall here, and up to nearly 400 inches had been recorded. Two National forests, Ottawa and Hiawatha, were located here. Towering, endless forests bordered the highway. Beautiful streams and the occasional waterfall were commonplace. A wildness had been slowly building the past few days as we got closer and closer to this place. I could feel it growing in me as well. Each day I left a little bit more of my socialized self behind and connected a bit more to the real. I no longer simply felt the road beneath my feet or the breeze across my face. I became them. It is an incredible connection and each day, in fact each step, provided an opportunity to connect more deeply.

As the miles passed by, my increasingly calm mind remembered a scene in *Dances With Wolves* when Kevin Costner danced around the fire outside his post with a tree branch spear in hand. Occasionally he stabbed a make-believe beast as he circled the giant blaze. I understood what he felt as he howled at the moon, circling the fire. He was leaving behind a part of himself that no longer served him. A naturalness, a wildness, was growing in him that could no longer be contained. It has always been one of my favorite scenes in the movie, and I was beginning to understand it more and more. I smiled, recalling the scene as I continued down the beautiful

Steven Cannon

stretch of road, occasionally howling at the pines and all that resided within them.

Day 22

Pee your pants and go back to bed forever.

Even the best-behaved, most well-mannered child sometimes blows up. Running nirvana is not without its bumps in the road. It was always exactly three steps from the foot of the bed in the RV to the toilet. This morning it seemed as though it was three hundred. It was a treacherous three steps, fraught with land mines, mental and physical. This morning the mental monologue began as soon as my eyes opened, probably even before. The key to taking those three steps was controlling the mind, focusing on only that *first* step. I would deal with the second step when it was time, but my mind was already way past that.

I'm not hungry, breakfast sucks everyday.
I'm tired of hating food every morning.
Hours and hours of running again today.
This is stupid.
Hope you're happy trying to be such a big shot.

Steven Cannon

One person can't make a difference anyway.
Today's the day your plantar fasciitis is gonna pop.
It's too far to the toilet. Just piss your pants and go back to bed...
forever.

The challenge just to sit up seemed monumental. *Shut the f$&k up, Steve, and sit up!* It was a full-on fist fight, and the best of me was getting the hell beat out of it. The screaming in my mind immediately drowned out any positive thought I could muster. I thought to myself, *How many damn voices are there in my head? Please make them stop!* I was on the verge of tears. I was not sure where all of this was coming from, but it felt as if I was imploding.

This mutiny was playing out on two fronts, the mental and the physical. Occasionally I could quiet the mind and make a slight break in its ranks. I'd then get blasted again by the physical, which would immediately knock me back to the mercy of my mind. There seemed to be an endless supply of ammo. Everything hurt. The tops of my ears hurt. I am nearly bald, but I swear, what little hair I had even seemed to hurt. The plantar fasciitis worked its way out each day as long as I gave my body plenty of time to warm up. I only needed to be gentle with my feet and let the blood start to flow, and I could run painless most of the day. Truly, the most dangerous part of each day was those first three steps to the toilet. *That's it!* I thought. *Just sit up, to hell with that, stand up on the bed and jump!* That should be sufficient to snap the tendons in both feet, and I could be done with all this madness.

This was going to take real cunning. I agreed to sit up as a step towards the jump-off-the-bed plan. If I could just sit up, I'd have a chance. From there I could make a break for freedom. I had fought this battle before but never to this extent. For the twenty one days prior, that first step to the toilet led to the second, which eventually

111

led to putting on one sock, then two. Then I would find myself drinking milk to push down the food in my mouth before I gagged on it. This would allow me to turn the RV door handle down towards the floor, releasing it open towards the world. Maybe the sun would be shining. I'd made it. I was sitting up for the twenty-second day in a row, perched at the end of the bed. A tear had found its way down my cheek. I wiped it away and got ready to take that first step. *Anyone can take just one step,* I reminded myself. *Anyone.*

The road proved challenging early. Running down the slightly slanted shoulder of a busy highway was no treat. The unnatural running angle jarred me with each step. There was no Lake Michigan nearby, which meant there was little to no breeze blowing off her cooling waters. This had a couple effects. One, it made things even hotter. The air was dead. It was similar to running in place in a steam room. I know that because I've done it. Some folks, while preparing for the Badwater 135, employ this particular training method to acclimate the body to running in temperatures that can approach 135 degrees or more. I have not yet taken on that beast of a race, but the temptation to try the workout was irresistible. At that moment it helped me mentally to reflect and think, *I've run in hotter conditions than this.* The other effect, which was impossible to prepare for, was the lack of wind that made navigation and attack much easier for the lethal Upper Peninsula mosquito. The ability to accept the heat, and even enjoy it, was a piece of cake by now. The mosquitoes required a bit more cover and some bug juice, but they were also manageable.

What I could not get out of my head was that a dear friend could be arriving at any moment. I had met Donna Lynch many years earlier on either RAGBRAI or Ride the Rockies. I couldn't recall for sure. It was safe to say we had logged many miles together on our bikes. She is a kindred spirit with a big thirst for adventure. She also possesses the kind of heart that chooses to hop on a plane from Colorado, fly to somewhere in Michigan, and rent a car to come find a friend and run with him for three days. I had nearly mastered the art of shutting down my brain but not today. Today it was allowed to play and watch the oncoming traffic to see if any of the cars were slowing, possibly to make a u-turn. I knew that her arrival, although very exciting and a reason for joy, also meant that she would have to leave. I put off the thought of that and rejoiced as a car pulled over in front of me and Donna jumped out. Hugs are a great thing. I consider myself a professional and take every chance I can to share one. I have to admit some do stand out. That was a great hug!

Day 23

Who might you inspire?

It was my Uncle Bob taking me to the Boundary Waters as a kid. It was my stepfather taking me out onto the Mississippi River hours before sunrise to hunt ducks. It was Rusty Bishop sharing his stories of endurance running all over the world. Amazing athletes, Lisa Smith Batchen and Marshall Ulrich blew my mind constantly with their beyond-human running adventures. When I look back, these were the people and events that watered the seeds of my soul that continued to grow out of control within me. I've come to believe that these seeds are carried by all of us. Some lie dormant, neglected and lacking the necessary ingredients to grow. Others, watered and basking in the sun from an early age, flourish to such a level that the origin is almost impossible to find. The beauty of this seed is that it never dies. *Never.* Given the slightest bit of nourishment, it wakes.

A person need only step outside on a clear evening in Colorado and look to the sky to feel it. Watch the sunset over the Badlands or simply breathe in deeply the scent of your freshly mowed lawn, and you will tap into it. We are meant to live big, step into the unknown, and take a juicy bite out of life.

It is never too early to start or too late to begin. Do not overanalyze. Set the goal and take the first step. Get the ball rolling. Let belief be your fuel. With each step, the dream gathers momentum, eventually becoming unstoppable. James Cameron was dead broke, living off of McDonald's coupons his mother sent him. He never lost faith while taking the necessary steps to bring *The Terminator* movie to life. To date, he has directed the highest grossing movie in history, *twice*.

These thoughts all rolled through my mind as we headed to meet the La Salle High School track team. Their coach had caught wind of our undertaking and wanted to bring his kids out to meet us. It was no surprise to find out the team was very successful; not every coach would take that sort of initiative. Their energy and smiles were infectious, full of wonderment. They asked many questions as did I. The girls' team had just dominated the Straights Area Conference meet, the boys a close second. Perhaps I would be a spark for one of these young runners. Maybe some of these eager young minds would someday look back and say that the guy running around Lake Michigan inspired them to train just a little harder or dream a bit bigger. That thought was incredibly humbling.

We had gotten a late start, our latest by far. It was one in the afternoon, but there were no regrets. Meeting the track team had been more than well worth it. I was nearly out the door when I realized I was missing just one thing. *I left them right there! I am sure of it!* "Where are my freaking headphones?!" my mind screamed. Or maybe it was out loud.

FORTY DAYS

I found out later that Jarred and Donna had delighted in my temper tantrum and had shared a good laugh at my juvenile fussiness after I exited the RV. It didn't seem very damn funny at the time. Donna's loan of her headphones kept me from a full-on meltdown. The blasting of music, the remote road, and the lush green trees lining it put the baby back into the basket. Occasionally the trees would break, allowing a glimpse of Lake Michigan. As always, it soothed me. It also revealed a better view of an increasingly darkening sky. Rain had been very scarce. These clouds seemed filled with bad intention.

As the road began to open up, so did the skies. The temperature dropped quickly as the sun was overtaken by the clouds. When the rain began to fall I immediately thought about ducking into the RV. The last three weeks in the sun had cooked me. The rain was now falling steadily, and the temperature had dropped nearly twenty degrees. *To hell with going into the RV.* I pulled off my shirt and immersed myself in the beauty of this storm. I thought of Tim Robbins's character in *Shawshank Redemption.* After crawling through a rancid sewer pipe to escape the prison, he ripped off his shirt and raised his arms to the sky as the rain cleansed his body and soul.

Donna, who had spent the past few hours catching up on work, was not going to miss out. While others in the county were heeding warnings of severe weather and heading for cover, Donna jumped out of the RV. We lasted three miles. By the time we finally succumbed, the winds were nearly blowing us off our feet, and the rain seemed to be coming from below us and above us at the same time. The RV door just about came off its hinges as we opened it to escape the storm. We joked about seeing flying cows and a lady riding her bike through the air with a dog she called Toto.

We found refuge in a nearby state park. Nine miles left, and the forecast was for storms to continue until midnight. The thought of having to make up nine miles on top of the usual twenty-six the next day was not an option. I mean, it was, but it wasn't. The state park, it turned out, had a sweet trail system. I reasoned the chance of being struck by lightning or snatched up by a tornado was far less in the woods. Falling limbs or trees I decided to not consider. The woods would wrap me in their arms and shield me from the dangers of the outside world.

The trails were covered in months, maybe years, of pine needles. It was as if I was running on sponges. With each step, the earth floor seemingly pulled the soreness from my aching legs. My pace began to quicken. The storms raged. I only needed to look up to see the treetops fighting to keep me safe. My breathing had found a rhythm. My legs were light and fresh. These woods were not just providing safety. It was as if they had spoken to the Great Lake and let her know they would take care of me in her absence. Her healing waters were temporarily replaced by the forgiving earth floor. I was eleven again, running home from school. I was a ghost through the woods. I was free of limits, running at a pace beyond what I should have been capable of. Turn after turn, hill after hill, my steps were effortless. I was flying. The rain, pouring from the sky, was being released gently onto me from the canopy. The winds, raging outside, were reduced to a cool, pine-scented breeze.

The storms continued well into the night. They broke from time to time which allowed Jarred to once again prepare a feast. We shared an incredible meal outside and recounted the great events of the day. It had certainly been one of the best. The skies were

FORTY DAYS

clearing when I excused myself to bed. Temperatures had dropped into the fifties. Jarred and Donna were still enjoying the beautiful evening as I tucked myself into bed. We were one happy, running, adventurous family. Drifting off to sleep, the headphone temper tantrum from earlier in the day seemed worlds away. Almost funny. Okay, very funny.

Day 24

Maybe all one needs is the connection.

Calories. Calories. Calories. It has been said that ultra-running is less a run than it is a drinking-and-eating contest. I was not involved in a race. Time was on my side. The Forrest Gump rules were in full effect. When I wanted to run, I ran. When I wanted to eat, I ate, and when I needed to go, well, you know, I went.

This morning, and on the many that preceded it, I lost the eating contest. My inability to eat much in the morning led to having to eat many more *shot blocks* than usual later in the day. I was consuming the gummy bear-like energy chews *en masse*. So many, in fact, that they had started to eat back. The inside of my cheeks felt like I was one block away from burning a hole right through my face. The pain in my cheeks gave me an even better reason to duck out on the morning breakfast ritual of *chew, chew, chew, don't hurl, don't hurl, don't hurl, wash it down, repeat*. I'd deal with the "bonk" when it came, if it came. I just said *"F" it!!* All I wanted to do was run.

119

FORTY DAYS

The prior day's storm had gifted us with much needed rain, which provided great relief from the heat and the bugs. People joke that the Michigan state bird could be the mosquito. They are *huge*. Although my appetite was missing in action, the mosquitoes certainly hadn't been suffering from the same. I was glad they were gone for now. Conditions were ripe to steal some comfy miles.

It wasn't storming at the start of the day, but the rain was coming. As is often the case, storms after prolonged heat waves are intense. Donna and I found another wonderful trail to run on. Sheltered by an endless forest of towering pines, we felt quite safe. If you have spent time in these kinds of places you know the smell. You can close your eyes at this very moment, breathe in deeply and return to that place. That place where you stood carefree amongst the pines and soaked in their scent. It's a smell that brings a smile to my face just thinking about it.

My feet, then calves, legs, and hips took to the kindness of the trail instantly, which in turn brought joy to all parts of my being. *Breathe in, breathe out. In. Out.* Observing my thoughts, detached from them, my mind began to quiet. Donna was the perfect mate because she too realized that at this moment conversation would just be noise. The quieter I became the more I began to connect with everything around me. I was no longer running on the ground but with the ground. It was not the wind from the pines that I felt but rather their life-giving breath.

The rain began to fall, and the cooling breeze began whipping up again. The rain became stronger, and the treetops started to howl. This storm was going to be the real deal. Maybe too real, I thought. My fear and concern for safety did not last long. It was as if Mother Nature held me in her arms. I could feel her. I was safe inside those woods, and they were my cradle. I was free to run. It felt as though

Steven Cannon

the woods, this place, existed solely to protect me, to see me safely through on my journey. I can only imagine what I looked like to anyone who could have seen. Shoes, shorts, no shirt, a well-worn bandana around my neck and a beard that was getting as wild as the surroundings. I was soaked head to toe, howling at the top of my lungs, completely out of my mind.

The miles that day passed faster and easier than any of the twenty-six miles on any of the twenty-three days that preceded them. Maybe shot blocks and breakfast were overrated. Maybe all one needs is the connection. I liked that thought.

Day 25

Friends are treasures.

Donna Lynch brought endless joy and energy to our two-man crew. Her enthusiasm extinguished any whining or negativity before it could even get started. She more than made up for the breeze that was missing from the lake. Truly, she was a giant gust of fresh air. We enjoyed miles of running together; sometimes she shared stories, other times just energy and space. We ran in the hottest of days and also got caught out in a storm that spawned more than one *Wizard of Oz* reference. She brought laughter and companionship into the RV for Jarred, which I'm sure was much needed. She cooked, she danced, she helped with needed errands, and she occasionally showed up with a stupid toy or two. She appreciated a good day on the road and wasn't afraid to kick her feet up by the fire and enjoy a whiskey with Jarred to celebrate another day in the books.

Where had the time gone? How could we be on our last "Donna Day"? What a trooper she had been, especially today. If it was possible for the humidity to be over 100%, today was that day. Two straight days of rain had soaked the earth, and now, without a cloud in the sky, it was nearly unbearable. My radar was up from the start: this day would be dangerously hot. We had not yet had to deal with this level of humidity combined with near-100 degree temps.

Heat exhaustion is a sneaky foe, lulling you slowly to sleep. The temperature started somewhere in the eighties, but by mile sixteen I realized I was in trouble. Donna had been along for every sweat-soaked mile. We stopped near a creek as we entered the town of Benton Harbor. I was crouching near the cool flowing creek when I nearly toppled over into it face first. *Wow*, I thought, *this is not good.* I'm not sure I could have gone much further, and I'm glad I didn't have to find out. It took several minutes of soaking my bandana and rubbing it all over my body before I began to regain lucidity. No doubt my brain was frying like an egg. I'd always let myself out of the steam room workouts way before this point. Wanting to capture the moment, I hit the record button on my iPhone. It was difficult to even form a thought. Donna hung in every single mile.

We finished the day together on a black asphalt bike trail that was way too damn hot for either of our tastes. We joked that it is always the challenging days, the really hot or really rainy, windy days that you remember. Those are the ones you talk about around the campfire. We'd had both. Tomorrow I'd have to deal with my friend being gone. I wasn't sure how my mind would handle that and I was in no hurry to find out. Certainly, it would be less than pleased. For now, those thoughts could wait.

The trees lining the parking lot provided a nice relief as we sat reflecting on the day. Our conversations were interrupted as cheerful music, not heard since our youth, found our ears. Had you asked me moments before, I would have told you that such things no longer existed. I was glad friends were there to confirm the event or in my state I may have thought it a mirage. It was an ice cream truck. A *real* damn ice cream truck! There was not a child served before or after that day who could've been more joyous than our crew. We rushed to that truck as if all of us were ten years old again. We couldn't have planned the day's end better had we tried.

We stayed at a hotel instead of the RV that night. A knock at the door meant an extra large pizza with all the toppings it could hold had arrived to our climate-controlled hotel room. All were compliments of Donna. She was not open to negotiations.

Day 26

I am mind. Hear me roar!

SHUT UP! To which I responded, *No, you shut up!* To which it had this to say: *I was doing just fine, sleeping like a baby, and you woke me up so now you gotta just f'n deal with it cuz I ain't going back to sleep! AND I got plenty to say!* The *it* was my brain.

Weeks before, I had fought through the wall, and there was a serene place on the other side. I knew from previous adventures that the quieting of the mind was not easy or enjoyable stuff. Everyday life is filled with so much noise, and our brains feed off of it. It becomes used to that noise. It *needs* that noise. When we go away for a few days on vacation, the brain takes a deep breath and almost lets us be. It could also be argued that all we really did was change the type of noise. Stay on that beautiful beach by yourself long enough, and you will have to deal with an inner revolt. That everyday noise becomes an addiction; take it away, and the mind gets the shakes. It goes through withdrawal, and you have two choices.

FORTY DAYS

One, go back to the noise, back to sleep. Two, breathe deep, hold on with all you got and pass through to the other side. It's a real challenge, but you'd be amazed at the peace that waits for you.

Donna had been the most beautiful noise. Yet, my brain took to her like an addict's would to their drug of choice, given the chance. I knew the risk. I knew spending time with her on the road would reawaken my mind. I just didn't realize to what extent. It was that way with everyone who joined us on the run. Their joy and enthusiasm were always welcome, but the emptiness that followed their departure was nearly unbearable.

Here I was, alone on the trail, and my mind was ready to go on a real bender. I've dealt with addiction in my life, and in many ways this was similar to the relapses I had seen up close. I had allowed myself to drink freely from Donna's bar. It was always happy hour with her in our midst. And now, just like that, she was gone. The lights were on, and someone was screaming, "Closing time! You don't have to go home, but you can't stay here."

How can that be?! my brain yelled, none too happy. *She just got here, we've all been having so much fun. We're not ready to stop. I want MORE.*

SHUT UP! I said. *Not this time,* my brain responded. *I've got lots to say. You realize you are all alone now, right? Still about 400 miles to go, right? How's that plantar fasciitis? Sure is hot! You're never gonna make it. 600 miles is a good run, and no one would hold it against you if you stopped here. Why don't you just quit?*

I could see Jarred up ahead, waiting as he always did. Two miles down, twenty-four to go. *Breathe...breathe.*

126

Day 27

All who seek, find.

A complete stranger wakes up in Traverse City, Michigan. After rolling out of bed to greet the day, she sits down with her coffee, checks a few emails, and then finds herself immersed in an article about a man attempting to run around Lake Michigan. Do you believe in fate or do you believe we are all just randomly bouncing around in this life, one "accident," one coincidence after another?

Angela Josephine is the kind of person who believes in fate. At her best, she not only notices omens, but also recognizes them as messages from the universe and acts upon them. Luckily for me, on this day she was at her best.

The struggle with my mind continued. I was at least two different people. At times it seemed like many more. The run served many different inner beings. I was always wondering, *Am I running towards something or away from something?* Was I running to find myself or was I running from myself? I had so loved Donna's com-

127

pany, and yet I thirsted to retreat inward again. I yearned for the peace and solitude the adventure provided, yet I could not deny that my love for people, known and unknown, was growing everyday. Solitude increased my connection to the *all*. The quiet space allowed for an even deeper connection with my truer self. In turn, this connection allowed for a deeper connection with people I met. At times I felt on the brink of crazy, but there could be no turning back. Back no longer existed for me. I was on my way to another so-called chance meeting, a wonderful coincidence.

My journey led me to a paved bike trail bordering a highway that would take me into Traverse City. It was a beautiful day. A hot air balloon danced among the clouds. The skyline of the city beckoned, and the trail became a bit busier with each mile.

Angela did what most people wouldn't have. She wanted to meet this runner guy; she had all the reasons to. Her cancer story, I would come to find out, bordered on the surreal; seemingly everyone in her family was fighting that damn disease. She loved to run. She loved adventure and yearned for more of it in her life, but she didn't even know this guy. She probably thought, *Would he want my company? He's probably really fast.* (A common misconception.) *What are the chances I'll even find him? I don't even know when he started today. He could be anywhere.*

Omens are a funny thing. One needs to meet them somewhere in the middle. They are merely a clue, a signpost that reads, "This way if you dare follow your heart." Many of us heed to the voices of safety, real or perceived. However, if you follow your heart and trust the omens, you will begin to tap into the reality that there are no accidents, no coincidences. Your omen radar will tune better and better, leading you on the life path you were born for. It does require a bit of effort and faith, but the rewards are a lifetime of joy and a death that will bring few, if any, regrets.

Angela Josephine chose to follow her heart and set out to find the tall balding man, hoping that someone who had been on the path for twenty-seven days would have a certain "look" to him. It had been some time since we had been into a town of any size. The trail was busy as I approached the outskirts of Traverse City. My mind was at peace. I looked right into the eyes of each passerby, hoping they felt my love for them. I didn't need to know them. I knew they were perfect. Each was on their own journey to somewhere, and I was happy to be sharing in that space. Some connected with my gaze, and we "saw" each other. Others passed without looking up, immersed in whatever they were immersed in.

Then, there she was. Of course I didn't know her. How could I? I couldn't even tell if she was a her. It would be more accurate to say I felt her. She was looking for someone, or maybe something. That was clear. She was taking an interest in those in front of me as they passed her. Most would not have noticed, but I did.

Our eyes met before our voices ever could have. I knew she was looking for me, or so my ego thought. In reality, there was a bit of truth in that. However, I would find out over the next sixteen miles we spent together that it was not me she came out to find but herself.

I spent much of the next many hours listening to her story and answering a few questions when asked. I would come to find out that Angela, like most of us, is a seeker. She hears the call of her soul and wonders if and how she will follow it. I'd like to think she found an answer or two that day on the trail. I was better for the experience and was grateful for her love, kindness, and openness.

FORTY DAYS

What a different day it would have been had she listened to all the reasons not to step out that morning.

Thank you, Angela, for following your heart.

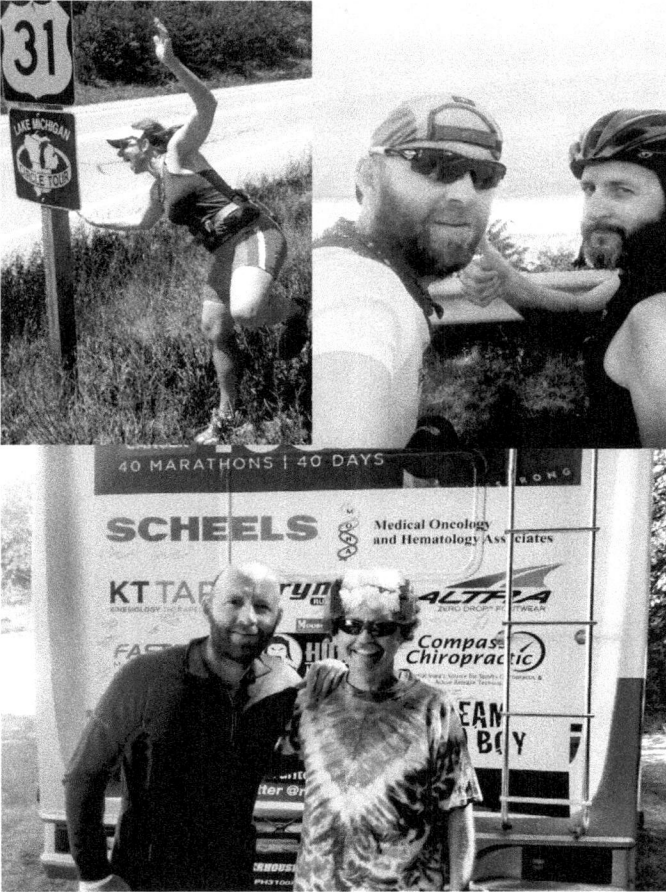

Top Left: Donna Lynch
Top Right: My Man Paco
Bottom: Terry Cury (aka The Grey Ghost)

Top Left: When I Was Tired, I Slept (Gump Rules)
Top Right: Jarred, The Man Never Left My Side (And Some
Crazy Lady)
Bottom: "Nothing Left"

Top Left: My Brothers in Adventure
Top Right: Chasing the Sun Into Night
Bottom: How I Really Feel About Cancer

Top Left: Hottest Memorial Day in Chicago History (Day 1)
Top Right: Me and Mom Hug "The Finish...Home"
Bottom: Jamie DeHayes "Gone Too Soon"

Top: Steve Falck and I with Chicago in Our Sights
Bottom: Mother Natue Welcomes Us Home

Day 28

The Grey Ghost

A few years ago, during my run across Iowa, I received a message: "Hi, Steve. My name is Terry Curry, and I am part of a group called the Muscatine Running Friends. We have been watching your run across Iowa, and if you can make it a few more days, we'd love to join you on the last day's run to the Mississippi River." I had no idea who Terry nor the Muscatine Running Friends were, but having more friends is never a bad thing. Terry, nicknamed the Grey Ghost or "GG" if you were in his inner circle, became a great friend.

Those final twenty-six miles or so into Muscatine on the final day of the Iowa crossing were magical. The Friends were a big part of that. What a great group they were, all brought together by their love of running. They stayed with me every step of the way, doing Muscatine proud. We shared stories, well, the GG shared most of them. That dude can story his way through a run of any distance.

FORTY DAYS

Years later, I would find out that he could stack day after day of stories, non-stop if you let him. That day was everything that was great about running. My effort to run across our wonderful state of Iowa had inspired them. In turn, their love of running and of others who loved running inspired me. The day had nothing to do with personal records, splits, or how many minutes that last mile took. Certainly these things have their place, but I believe they have greatly watered down all the wonderful things a run can offer.

We were fully immersed in the running experience. The nearly unbearable heat had broken just a few days prior. We basked in the cool temperatures and the cover of the clouds. There was always time for a pit stop, be it for food, drink, or a trip into the corn-field. Stories of past races and running adventures were shared by all. The Friends spoke of their annual Christmas run. They reveled in all their running adventures, and it was a joy to be a spectator: how fast some people were, how others were new to the sport—just finding their legs—and how no one really cared. This was more of a family than a running group. It was beautiful to see how they all admired and looked out for one another, always full of encouragement.

The GG had a quick wit and a dry humor that I took to quickly. He was a generous, kind-hearted man as well. There also seemed to be an adventurous side to him. If there was a run to be had he was ready for it, be it in freezing cold, in the rain, close to home, or far away, the wackier the better. I was looking forward to seeing him again.

Jarred had found us a sweet little hideaway the night before be-hind a little church that neither of us could decide for sure was in business. Not because it was old or rundown, far from it. It was perfect, in a century-old-maybe-would-hold-thirty-people sort of way. It was one of our favorite activities, playing vagabond at the end of each day, trying to scrounge up a place to stay. We were batting near 100%. Our method of driving around at ten miles per hour, looking for a place to pull in for the night caught the attention of a few locals one evening, and the police paid us a visit. Fortunately for us, they believed the "We are trying to run around Lake Michigan" story. Who would make that up? We enjoyed a pretty good laugh after thinking, had we indeed been thieves in the night, why would we choose a vehicle with the stealthiness of a 1998 RV? On second thought, maybe the absurdity of it would have made it the perfect vehicle. We looked at each evening's treasure hunt for a place to call home as a challenge, always attempting to set a new high...or low.

The church lot was on the high end of the scale. It was clean, which was a plus. The grounds were dimly lit, which made for better sleeping. And finally, the pavement was level. This was a VERY important detail. I wasn't the only one always exhausted at day's end. Twice, our haste in finding a spot to park the RV for the night led to us waking up with our faces pasted to the wall because we had unknowingly settled on an incline or tilt in the rush to close our eyes.

I awoke to discernible mumbling and a bit of laughter. Once the cobwebs cleared enough to realize I was actually awake and not dreaming, the pieces slowly started to come together. It seemed to me as if I had just fallen asleep. It always felt that way. Clearly, the morning was not still new. The sun, in addition to the *two* people yucking it up outside confirmed that. I knew that he was on his way. We had been in contact off and on since before the start of the run, and much more since he had made it to Michigan a couple days earlier. Truth is, since that first day spent running to the Mississippi River together, we had stayed in touch, shared a few more runs and became great friends.

I slowly got to my feet, stepped gingerly out the door and down the RV steps, and there was the Grey Ghost in all his splendor, rocking an awesome rainbow afro! There was no better food to start the day than a good laugh. He would be with us for the next three days. His plan was to take down a marathon each day at my side. I never allowed myself to think about Navy Pier in Chicago, where I would finish if successful, but I couldn't deny the feeling that it somehow felt just a little bit closer at that moment. Maybe even attainable.

Day 29

It's all in how you look at it.

In the movie *Groundhog Day*, Bill Murray wakes at the exact same time everyday to the exact same Sonny and Cher song, "They say we're young, and we don't know. We won't find out until we grow. Well I don't know if all that's true, 'cause you got me, and baby I got you." Somehow, he became trapped, living the same day over and over and over...and over again. It does not matter how he lives that day. He may choose to do good, bad, or nothing at all. Each night he falls asleep, and just like that, he's back exactly where he started. I could not help but notice the similarities in this journey I was on. No matter what had taken place the day before I would find myself sitting at the end of the bed in the RV, contemplating how the hell I would make it three steps to the toilet. This thought was not accompanied by Cher, unfortunately.

What Bill Murray's character eventually came to realize was that the same exact day can take on an entirely different quality based on one's attitude. He was, for the most part, a miserable man. He had a job he disliked and a life that had been up to this point lacking in fulfillment. He held no compassion or love in his heart for others. In actuality, he seemed to find a bit of pleasure in the simple act of sharing unpleasantries. The only thing worse for him would be getting stuck in a small miserable town in Pennsylvania, reporting on a groundhog's verdict of winter vs. spring, for eternity. Everyday would be that day.

I had plenty of reasons to bitch and moan. Every muscle in my legs was a wreck. I had plantar fasciitis in both feet that threatened to pop every morning during these first few steps. If the pilgrimage to the pisser was successful, my payoff was a breakfast that would gag me, waiting on the other side of the door. Jarred would be doing everything he could to help me get rolling. I hated help when I didn't want help. GG was up and ready to go, cracking jokes, happy as a lark. I hated happy people when I didn't want to be happy. Oh yeah, and I had to go knock out another twenty-six miles or so for the twenty-ninth consecutive day. *Probably another 90 degree furnace out there again,* I thought, still perched on the bed's end. Paralyzed by my thoughts, I had yet to take step one towards relieving myself of this overly full bladder. *This sucks.*

In *Groundhog Day,* Bill Murray's character took quite a ride. He decided to take advantage of the situation and everyone in it. He ate everything in sight, became more rude, and even took advantage of a lady or two. *Why not?* he thought. He even seemed to find pleasure in it for awhile, but the joy was fleeting. It eventually led to a deep depression, and he tried everything to get out of the loop, even suicide. That didn't work either. No matter his choices, each day began with him in the exact same bed, the exact same radio alarm clock playing the exact same song, and the exact same opportunity facing him. *There it was!* The word was not one he had used or recognized before. Each day had seemed to be many things—difficult, depressing, hopeless, worthless—but *never* seemed to be a day of opportunity. This day was exactly the same, but this time he wasn't.

He snapped out of bed, left the room neatly dressed and freshly shaved. Immediately, all the events of the seemingly endless loop appeared differently to him. He couldn't wait to get downstairs, say his "hellos", get to the café, and meet his coworkers. He took an extreme interest in every situation. Each person he encountered got his very best response. He realized that what was once a heavy burden, at times too much to bear, was in reality a great gift. He had an unlimited number of days in which he could better himself and share that with all those around him. Each day was a fresh chance to spend time with this person or that. He spent day after day trying to save the homeless fellow down the street. He learned to play the piano and become an expert ice sculptor. Eventually he fell in love, and just like that, he was free. Life began again anew.

It's amazing how many thoughts can travel through your mind while frozen on the end of a bed, unable to move, trying to figure out how to get up and just go pee. *Opportunity.* That's what I had at that moment. From an outsider's view, the upcoming day would look almost exactly the same as the last day. There was no denying each day had a ritualistic look to it. Rise, run, sleep, repeat.

The word *opportunity* changed that moment for me, which in turn set the wheels in motion for a wonderful day. It was a valuable lesson learned from that seemingly benign comedy film. The circumstances in our life do not dictate the quality of our experience.

FORTY DAYS

If we view each encounter as an opportunity, a chance to offer the best we have, we get the best out of each circumstance in return.

Suddenly, I found myself excited for the day ahead. It had only been a few minutes sitting in contemplation on the end of the bed, but the entire day would now be a completely positive experience, starting with those same first three steps. The exact same three steps from every day prior would now be different.

Day 30

Make today a great movie.

Day Thirty passed quickly. It's funny how time works. What had once seemed so far away, comes and goes and leaves you pondering where the time went. It had been seventy-two hours and three marathons since the rainbow-afro'd man known as the Grey Ghost had awoken me with his laughter. He had ran, walked, and shuffled along with me, somehow making time just disappear.

Someday, I believe, death will meet me with a gentle kiss and a welcoming bear hug. There will be no pain, no fear, just a loving greeting to the next realm. A beautiful peace and knowing that everything is exactly as it is supposed to be will color all that is. Just before this welcoming, I will be able to watch the movie of my life unfold before me. The most poignant and beautiful times will play out again. Death will wait patiently, as it exists in a timeless place. It will be in no hurry. Maybe it, too, will find joy in the feature film. These last few days had been filled with many moments that would make such a movie's final cut.

GG's never-ending stories and jokes kept the mind occupied and, at times, too busy. Early on, the input was more than my previously serene mind could take: too much of a good thing. I would drop back behind the Ghost and occasionally mutter "uh huh," while enjoying the quiet my headphones provided. It was no problem. Every five or ten minutes, I'd pull them out just to check on him. All was good. He was still chatting away.

At one point, his storytelling and my attempt to disconnect for a bit were suddenly interrupted. GG made a sudden big leap out into the road, not the smartest thing to do, but the exact kind of thing anyone would do upon noticing a couple skunks immediately to their left. A subconscious thought: being sprayed by skunks is a greater evil than being flattened by oncoming traffic. We got lucky on two fronts. There was no oncoming traffic, and the skunks held no ill will toward runners. Maybe they liked GG's ramblings. We didn't hang out to test that theory. I also realized that after twenty-nine days my legs could move damn fast with the proper motivation. Man, was I glad they didn't spray us. We no sooner thanked the gods for our good fortune when it happened again! Apparently, we had stumbled onto the Skunk Capitol of Michigan. Perhaps I was unknowingly running with some kind of skunk Pied Piper. We would have close encounters with three skunk packs over about a five-mile stretch. None saw fit to let us have it, although all were close enough to do so. It was unreal that we got away unskunked.

There was no way of knowing that the kiss of all kisses awaited as the GG and I turned onto a country road. Even as we got closer to the beautiful farm house there was no reason to suspect such a thing. Obviously a party of some sort was going on. There were tons of cars and trucks parked on the long driveway, and the music was kicking. No way we were not going to investigate this and seize the chance to make new friends.

We walked slowly up the driveway and were greeted halfway by the family that lived there. They were very interested in what we had going on as well. *What was up with the slow moving RV with the sponsor logos on it? The two guys running down the road? Where ya coming from? Headed to?* They had questions, and the Grey Ghost was quite the PR guy. Fresh ears were like crack to that guy.

With all the commotion surrounding us, it was easy not to notice him. He was in no hurry, but I did catch a glimpse of him as our guests continued their inquisition. The beast was headed straight for me. His pace quickened as he got closer. His energy was enormous. Perhaps he sensed some of the same. I couldn't wait for him to get to me. Whatever was being said at that moment between our new friends and the GG faded away.

Slowly, so as not to startle, I lowered myself to the ground and extended my arms. He was in a full trot now, and I could see he had nothing but love in those huge, droopy eyes. Thor was a giant of a mastiff. He barreled into me, perhaps sensing the joy in my heart. It was such a pure encounter. He damn near drowned me in slobber as I held on with all I had. It felt as though I could have hugged that beast forever. Each moment charged my battery more and more. I hoped somehow that big ole brute was feeling the same. I can't be sure how long we rolled around. Time just sort of vanished. Eventually, we had to say our goodbyes and continue on our journey. They let us know, if ever back in their neck of the woods, we should plan on staying a bit longer. There was a real genuineness to the offer.

FORTY DAYS

We found other expressions of support along the route. A smile from a well-wisher, a honk and a thumbs up, a text message, or voice mail all helped buoy the soul. I was so raw, so opened up from the journey, that even these seemingly simple gestures would at times make me shed a few tears. Everything meant so much more now. Each connection was felt more deeply. I would soak in every encounter. It provided to my spirit the same soothing effects the lake provided to my physical body.

We knew we were nearing the end of the day. The mind becomes quite the GPS after 700 miles of running. The GG was somewhere between story forty-three and ninety-six, there was no way to know the exact number. It seemed he had perfected the art of storytelling, while somehow simultaneously running and breathing. The upcoming hill was to put the old boy to the test. We were nearing an area known for its sand dunes, which were rumored to be enormous. To our right we noticed a change in the landscape. The forest was becoming more sparse. The land itself was changing in appearance, and the normally flat terrain had taken a turn towards the sky. It is a "suggestion" in ultra-running races that if you can't see the top of a hill, walk it. We would have none of that. I thought, *If this old bird walks, I'll walk,* but I wanted to give it a go. I'm guessing his inner dialogue was something like *This guy's on Day Thirty; if he ain't walking, I damn sure ain't.* In truth, most people could have walked it faster than we ran it. The road twisted and turned its way upward until Jarred and the RV finally appeared. We knew that would be the top. It was a cool moment. We shared a glance: no need to talk, even if we could have. Still very much in the moment, after time to catch our breath, we asked Jarred how much further. "You're done boys. Great job!" We hugged, high-fived, and made for the RV, excited for dinner and real beds at the Grey Ghost's friends' place.

"You guys may want to turn around before we leave," Jarred suggested. In our haste, joy, and exhaustion, we had nearly missed out. It seemed the entirety of Michigan lay behind and below us. The word awesome was made for views like this. It was as if we had climbed the beanstalk. We were, for the moment, giants. Thank goodness for Jarred...again.

The next morning, Jarred and I would be embarking on Day Thirty-One. The Ghost would not be joining us. His running legs needed to transition quickly to sea legs. Our hosts for the past two nights had been Eric and Marilyn Walline from Gold Coast Deep Sea Fishing in Frankfort, Michigan. Eric was an old high school buddy of the Grey Ghost. Not surprisingly, they were great hosts. It was easy to see how the two of them had been lifelong friends. Based on the kindness and generosity they showed our crew, I had no doubt their charter fishing service was quite successful. It never failed; everyone who put us up was always so full of excitement. They opened their lives to us, making us feel like long lost family returning home. Sitting together after dinner, my mind wandered. I began to reflect on the past few days. How could it have gone so fast? It is said that all good things come to an end. I don't know about that. If those things or people remain in our memory, in our hearts, do they ever really end?

Day 31

If today were your last day...

It is hard to imagine it. What would your reaction be? "Your results are back. Your cancer is very advanced. There is nothing we can do." The natural response, I suppose, is "How long....how long do I have left?" I do not know how my Uncle Mike responded. "One, maybe two weeks," is the reply he received today.

Take a moment, and put yourself in that hospital bed. Feel those words being said to you: "One, maybe two weeks." What would you do? What feelings would be foremost? Sadness, despair, fear, anger, panic, denial, disbelief, shock. Who would be the people you would reach out to first? Are there things left unsaid to those you care for? People you could forgive? Including yourself. "One, maybe two weeks." That's the time you have been given. Does today look any different to you now?

Every morning, without fail, I had woken up to a text message joke from my mom. No such message waited for me this morning. It was not until the phone rang that I understood why. Mom shared the news with me about Uncle Mike.

I could tell Mom was shaken. She tried her best to not let on, wanting to stay upbeat for her son. She said things like, "Don't worry, I'll be ok. It's gonna be alright. We'll just have to do our best." This would be Mom's second sibling whom cancer had taken. A month earlier, they had been trying to figure out what was causing Uncle Mike to feel so crappy. Just a week ago he had been diagnosed, and they were hopeful that he would be able to mount a defense and fight the disease. Now, the doctors were dismissing him. The latest results showed the body beyond repair. The cancer so advanced there was nothing that could be done. "Days...a week, maybe two."

What would you do? Who would you call? Where would you go to spend your last days? Who would you invite?

The answer to where he would go was an easy one. Lost Island Lake was the place for Uncle Mike. It was his heaven on earth, the place he had always felt most alive. His family and closest friends had spent countless days and evenings there together. If there was any way that he could get there, that would be his wish. To spend his last days with those he loved in his favorite place.

There was much to be done and not much time. Tomorrow was not a guarantee. A hospital bed was needed; medications and information on how to administer them and getting Uncle Mike there comfortably were just a few of the issues. Somehow the family rallied to make sure Uncle Mike would get his wish. If it was the lake he wanted, he was damn sure gonna get it.

They made sure the cabin was perfect. The bed had a view of the lake. Lights were strung up outside. One last lake party for Uncle Mike was planned. His family all gathered, friends also. Uncle Mike slept most all of the time, the medications to keep him out of pain were strong. It was as happy a time as it could be considering the circumstances. Uncle Mike had always been the life of the party. His wonderful life energy was noticeably missing.

The family decided to back off the medication a bit to see if perhaps he might wake for awhile and be able to join the party, and enjoy it, even if just for a short time.

Slowly, he began to wake and become more and more coherent. Were it not for him laying in a special bed provided for his comfort and his obvious weakened state, he was good ole Uncle Mike again. He was not one to miss a lake party, and for the moment, it was apparent, he had been given a window of time to enjoy this one.

"Maybe we should take the boat out for a cruise," he said. For a moment, all was right in the world. The suggestion rallied everyone. Uncle Mike was back! Of course, everyone knew this was probably the last cruise they would all ever take together. That mattered little at that moment. When Captain Mike said one last go, the crew was all hands on deck.

The boat was brought to the dock, fueled up, and ready to go. Family and friends gathered all around. Uncle Mike, too weak to move on his own but fully alive in every way, was carried from the cabin to the boat in the arms of his brother. A more intimate, beautiful moment I cannot imagine.

The pontoon boat was probably rated to hold six to eight people. Once Captain Mike was lowered into his seat, the number was probably twice that. At that moment, there was no more cancer, no terminal disease. There was just a boat full of people enjoying a night on the lake with their favorite captain, who was all smiles just like he always had been. Someone worried that they may get stopped for having the boat overloaded. They joked, "That's okay, Uncle Mike's driving. The water patrol can give him the ticket! They're gonna have a tough time collecting on that one!" I'm sure Uncle Mike thought that was damn funny. We should all be so lucky to spend our last days surrounded by those we love in our favorite place.

Day 32

Look beyond. Believe beyond.

The day started with a tour of Arcadia, Michigan. Our hosts from the previous evening, Ted and Yolan (Yo) Leno, had rolled out the red carpet the night before. Arcadia is a beautiful, sleepy little town that sits right on Lake Michigan. The Leno's had a magnificent home and fed Jarred and me like kings. It was great to see Jarred on the receiving end of a great meal prepared by someone else. Like most nights, I was not the most social house guest. I'd do my best to answer questions and enjoy social time, but the call of a real bed, especially after gorging myself, always won out. There would be no dine and dash this morning though. Ted would not have that. After we polished off another wonderful meal at breakfast, Ted insisted on sightseeing. It was easy to tell he was very proud of his beautiful little town and wanted to show us a few highlights. We were happy to indulge him, confident the couple thousand calories we had packed away the last two meals would get us through the running later that day, regardless of our start time.

Ted saved the best for last. Not far outside Arcadia, we found ourselves on a two-lane very winding road. The road became quite steep, and around each corner I figured that would be the end. Eventually it was. That would not be the end of our climbing however. The sweet spot, Ted let us know, was still a little steep hike from the parking lot. I thought for a moment that hiking up a few hundred feet wasn't the best idea for these legs but what the hell. No way I was going to tell Ted no. Truth be told, the short hike sucked, but *Wow,* I thought, *it was worth it!* From the top, the view was astounding. I could not have imagined it from the parking lot not far below us. It reminded me once again of a favorite quote: "Go to the absolute edge of what you believe is possible. From there an entirely new view of possible awaits." Ted had given us one hell of a tour and finished it off in style. Gazing over what seemed like the entirety of Lake Michigan, my thoughts wandered. It had been an incredible journey to get here. I never could have imagined this life. It seemed so very improbable that I was the one here, now, in this place, on this adventure.

In 1998 I had just wanted to run a St. Paddy's Day 5k to meet chicks. I hadn't even liked to run. Certainly, I had spent much of my youth and early adult years running, but not physically. There are those who see their path at an early age and have a real sense of the destination. That was not me. I knew only one thing. The "real world" was not going to be my path. I am not entirely sure where this rebellious view came from. It may have been my anger and sorrow from my parents' divorce that fueled it. I remember my Dad saying after disappointingly looking over another one of my report cards, "Son, one of these days you're gonna have to wake up and get with the real world." That was his go-to warning anytime I stepped out of line. The more he went to it, the more I decided, *If the world goes left, I'm going right.* My path took many different turns. Many ended up being the wrong way down a one-way street. Yet somehow I was here, now, totally at peace with who and where I was.

The day passed easily. I didn't set any personal records, but the great rest and meals from our stay in Arcadia the night before set the stage for a day without land mines. The miles passed by one after another without incident. Day Thirty-two was in the books. Somewhere around 830 miles behind me was Navy Pier. A much more appealing thought, which I rarely allowed myself or anyone else to discuss, was that about 200 miles in front of me was Navy Pier, where I had started over a month ago. *Holy shit!* At that moment I realized I had been running for over a month. *How could that be possible? How does one go from chasing girls at a 5k to this?* It seemed like an absurd question. One that would typically be answered by, "You don't."

Anything is possible if you can see it. Remember that. There were times during the planning, the training, and even a few moments over the past thirty-two days that I hadn't been sure I could do it. That, however, has nothing to do with if it's possible. The moment I could see it, it became possible. If I chose to quit, that would be on me. I was so grateful to still be here, in the game.

It wasn't until the third or fourth 5k, so many years ago, that I could see the possibility of doing a 10k. I remember, very vividly, thinking to myself at the end of my first half-marathon, *Hell no. No freaking way could I turn around and run back to the start.* But after finishing my second one, I could see it. It had been there all along. I just hadn't been able to see it before. The marathon was visible to me. I had climbed to a height that allowed me to see more of what I was capable of.

Know this: you are capable of so much more than what you believe, than what you can see for yourself. There is an entire valley of greatness that lies in front of you, full of indescribable beauty and joy. Let that knowledge propel you to take on your next challenge and make that climb. The view will amaze you. Not just the view in front of you but also the one behind. Enjoy the space. Swim in it. You have earned it.

In time, something in the distance will catch your eye. For some, it will happen quickly; for others, a bit longer. It is certain to happen, for you are now an explorer on a journey without limits. There will be a higher peak that calls. A new challenge. A new adventure. You will welcome each new undertaking with more excitement and less fear, for the joy of the journey and the view from the next peak must be even grander.

We are creatures of unlimited potential. We need only dare to take the first step. Just one step allows us to see a little more of what is possible. We can see just a bit more of what lies ahead because of that step. Our possibilities are endless because we can always take one more step.

Day Thirty-two had passed almost without notice. Was it time compression? Had time become just a word? This place, without name, was becoming more and more my reality. I could now see the possibility. No, to hell with that. I could now see the probability of Day Thirty-three. What a beautiful view!

Day 33

A mother's love trumps all.

One word: *brutal.* I took one step out of the RV, and that was the word. There was no need to ask what the temperature was. It didn't matter. The mind and body tune in very well to certain things after thirty-two days and over 800 miles of running. I didn't need a GPS to tell me how far I had gone. Turn me loose, let me go, and at any time ask me how far we had come that day, and I'd be damn close. It was the same with the weather. We didn't speak much about Fahrenheit or Celsius. We were more descriptive than scientific. Subconsciously, I'm sure there was a process which led to this one-word thought. It all took just a few seconds and was not perceptible to my conscious mind. The inner dialogue probably chatted about how it felt a bit balmy right now and that there was very little breeze. It probably also observed the lack of cloud cover and the fact that we would be separated from the lake all day long, which eliminated her cooling. All of that took place without notice. The only word clear to me at that moment was *brutal*.

There was also one other slight anomaly. No morning joke again from my mother. Like all other things that occurred from time to time that were odd or uncomfortable, it too needed to be put on the mental back shelf.

The day we had started the run had been the hottest Memorial Day in Chicago history. Temperatures on the road had approached 120 degrees in the city that day. Since that day, very few mornings had begun with the words *nice* or *comfy*. I think it was Day Three or Four maybe, that the day started with a stocking cap and the word *chilly*. Thirty-two days were behind us and twenty-eight of them had been over ninety degrees, many at or near 100. The entire Midwest was experiencing a heat wave of historical levels, and today would be the hottest we had faced yet.

Jarred and I had to adjust our game. There would be no "go two miles, and I'll let you know when I get there if I need you." No "go on down the road ten miles, kick back, and I'll see you in a couple hours." Today would be self-defense. It wasn't going to be hot, it was going to be dangerously hot. The general public was being told, "If you don't need to be outside today, don't go. If you do go out, be very careful." Certainly, the weather forecaster, or anyone else for that matter, would strongly disapprove of running a marathon on completely exposed asphalt roads.

The temperature was rising much quicker than I could click off the miles. The lake was just a mile or so from us, but it may as well have been a hundred. We could not see her because of the woods that lay between us, and worse, much worse, we could not feel her. There was not even the slightest bit of cooling breeze. It was the perfect sauna. The air temperature and the sun were beating down on me, while at the same time cooking the asphalt below me. I could feel the heat from both directions. It seemed as if it was passing through my body to the asphalt, amplifying itself and returning though me twice as hot as before. The intensity of it all was both painful and intoxicating. I was at the absolute limit of what I was capable. It was taking me nearly fifteen minutes to cover each mile. By the time I reached the RV I could barely process any thought.

Who I was or where I was were imperceptible. I was in total survival mode. Any thought would be a waste of energy. Everything in me was spoken for. Get to the RV, cool, rehydrate, go again. Nothing else. Jarred would be waiting with the AC cranked. It too was being pushed to its limits. I'd enter the RV, close the door quickly behind me and slump in a heap onto the couch. Jarred would immediately go to work. New bandana filled with ice, check. Cold watermelon at my side, check. New dry socks if needed, Check. The list was long. He handled everything with ease. In my condition, left to my own abilities to process anything, it would have been impossible.

Then would come the most difficult part. Slowly, the AC would bring me back, and I had to get my ass up immediately or risk getting comfortable and not getting out again. Ever. I loved the challenge. It was unlike anything I had ever experienced. It was one of the reasons I had come here. To lose what did not serve me and find how deep inside I could go. I would enter the RV on the brink of collapse, and I would force myself back out the moment I sensed relief. Jarred and I were in the zone, a finely tuned machine, taking down one mile at a time, together, against the nastiest furnace you could imagine.

The zone was interrupted as my phone vibrated on the counter.

Steven Cannon

Someone was calling, which was unusual at this time of day. Words of encouragement came in great quantity but mostly at the start of each day. Words of congratulations and "almost theres" came toward the end of each day. It was an odd moment for the phone to buzz. Somehow, I knew. I could feel Mom on the other end of the phone before I ever saw her name. I also sensed something was terribly wrong. She has since told me that she nearly did not make the call. Her motherly instincts told her not to burden her son. He had all he could handle. Mom loved these adventures and hated them as well. She worried about my safety, and the heat wave did nothing to put her at ease. It had to be an enormously hard call to make, but I am glad she chose not to carry the pain alone.

Somehow I knew it before she uttered her first words. The subconscious had put it all together. There had been no morning funny text, no words of love and encouragement. Something had to be wrong.

"Hello sweetie. How ya holding up?" She said. Of course putting her concerns for her son first, even though she had just lost her second sibling to cancer. "Uncle Mike has died." From the time of his initial diagnosis he had been given a few months, then maybe a month, hopefully a couple weeks, and now just a week later, he was gone.

The run no longer mattered. Maybe it should have mattered even more at that moment, but it didn't. All that mattered was Mom. "I'm so sorry Mom. I'll come back to Iowa, the run can wait." Tears replaced the sweat flowing down my face. "You will do no such thing, young man. Uncle Mike knew what you were doing and was so proud of you. You need to finish this run. We all love you very much. I'll be okay. The whole family is here."

FORTY DAYS

"Okay, Mom. I will. I'm so sorry, and I love you so much."

"I love you too. You take care of yourself out there."

"I will. You, too"

I handed Jarred the phone and sobbed into the towels that covered my head. I was overcome by not only the sadness of Uncle Mike's death but again by the unconditional love of my mother. I'm not sure I will ever fully grasp the depths of love mothers hold for their kids.

Jarred held me in his arms for a few seconds as I continued to cry. We shared a knowing glance that now, more than ever, for Uncle Mike and for all the others who would get a call like this today, the run must keep moving forward.

"See you in a mile, Jarred."

"I'll be there," he said. He always was.

Day 34

Chugga Chugga, Chugga Chugga, Wooh Wooh!

There was an odd sense of things this morning. Something was different. Certainly, after thirty-three days of this journey, I had changed. Perhaps changed was not the correct term. It was not a change as much as a clean burn. Unneeded things had been discarded. Things that were once important or necessary were no longer so. Simplified. Yes, that was the word. I had been simplified, reduced to the real. Outside influences, once an integral part of my life, were now noise. Noise sensed by not just the ears but also the mind. Music had long since been replaced by the simple, yet far more beautiful, sounds produced by nature. Whereas before I might have heard the birds singing, the waves crashing on the lake, or the breeze swooshing through the trees, it was much more intimate now. I had become a part of these things. No longer were we separate. I could sense the connectivity of it all and my place in it.

Music, TV, the newspaper, the internet; noise, noise, noise, and noise. They were all a distraction from the real. They were things that I no longer had any desire for, nor gained any satisfaction from. The number one reason to adventure, to go beyond your comfort zone, is that with each mile, each hour, you uncover a bit more of who you are at your core. I wondered just how deeply I could go.

I thought to myself, *Maybe the crazy adventurous fools I admire don't go bigger each time to set new records or stroke their egos. Maybe each bigger adventure allows them to go further inside, to come closer to the ultimate face-to-face. Maybe the seemingly insane challenges are just a mechanism, a vehicle.* The Native Americans called it a vision quest, days spent in solitude with nature. It was a time of deep spiritual connection where one would have profound insights and find their place in the world. A place where there was no longer an "I" in the egotistic sense but rather the universal "I." A place where you just *are.*

I was closer to that place now than at any other time in my life. The miles, the heat, the love, and loss were all playing a part in the shedding of layer upon layer of bullshit. Suddenly my seven remaining days were not a challenge, but a concern. My time in this space was running out. I welcomed each day ahead of me. My body could continue on forever it seemed. Today would be an opportunity to go deeper into the *real.* It would provide another day to raise money, and maybe even inspire. Day Thirty-five would follow and Day Thirty-six after that, each offering the gift of further self exploration.

What happens when it's all over, then what? my mind chimed in. It never missed an opportunity to chime in. That was the end of the inner dialogue. The shoes were laced up. I had been fed and watered. Jarred would be waiting a couple miles down the road. I'd start out walking until the body was ready to quicken the pace. Sometimes it would take a mile, sometimes more. As the body warmed, the mind would quiet, and both the inner and outer journey would begin anew. *Where would today take me?* That one question provided the necessary fuel for each step; most importantly, for the first step.

Jane Alshouse Arpy and I had met years prior, but I'm not sure exactly where or when. Probably on a random bike ride back home in Des Moines. Perhaps RAGBRAI. I hope all my friends excuse my lack of memory in such matters and don't take it as a sign of not caring. It is certainly one of the qualities I wish was better in me. The thought of age making it even worse is not a pleasant one. Hopefully, my own name does not escape me any time too soon. It always impresses the hell out of me when people I have met recall my name and the circumstances of our initial meeting. That may become of great use to me in the future.

If all went according to plan, our day would end in Muskegon, Michigan. We would be twenty-six miles closer to our final destination and make the acquaintance of Danielle and David Snyder. Danielle was Jane's daughter. Their home would also be our home tonight. Jane had planned a visit there and set the whole thing up. The kindness and generosity of people on this trip never stopped. That is the way with adventuring. Everyone who has ever struck out will back me on this. Don't get too caught up in every little detail. The universe has got your back.

We took a break at the twenty-mile mark. I was not doing well. The boiler room was screaming for more coal. The reserves were not there. Muskegon was in sight so we chose to drive into town, meet our hosts real quick and hopefully get some coal back into the boiler. Mind and body were both empty. It sure was tempting to just stay in Muskegon and say "f@#k it". Driving into town was probably not a good decision. Eating and drinking just didn't seem to do the trick this time. Another wall had appeared, and this one was the real deal. The thought of driving back out of town to finish up the day was almost enough to bring an emotional meltdown. Jarred knew I was in a deep funk. By this time in our adventure, he always knew when I needed space and when I needed a shoulder to lean on or a pep talk. I was grateful for the quick talk. His words were not new, but they were timely.

I swung the door open. *It's okay,* I told myself. *We've got plenty of time* (we being all the voices and differing personalities within). *If we gotta walk these last six miles, that's what we'll do.* With that first step, I knew I had done it. I'd make it through the day. I would finish those last six miles. Jarred returned to town to take care of a few things. I assured him all was good. The walking lasted for less than a mile. My pace quickened to a shuffle. I could feel it happening. The coal, in such short supply only hours before, was now seemingly plentiful. I pictured a great steam engine, the wheels slowly gaining speed, the smokestack starting to billow. My breathing began to quicken as did my pace. This train was starting to roll and was beyond me to slow down. I was becoming a spectator of myself. It is a difficult thing to explain. Euphoria, Nirvana, out-of-body, it was all of these. I was free of all physical and mental limitations. Pure joy, absolute freedom.

There was no real way to explain to Jarred what had happened when he eventually tracked me down. I had ran well beyond the six miles needed, and were it not for our social responsibilities in

Muskegon, I would have ran many more. It was easily one of, if not the best, run of my life.

Jarred pulled the RV up alongside the curb. He gave a few quick honks of the horn to announce our arrival. Tucker, a beautiful Husky mix, was set on leading the welcoming committee. As we exited the RV he launched out of the patio window four feet off the ground, tongue ready for anyone who wanted a big sloppy "Welcome to my house" kiss. His buddy Owen, also a Husky mix, chose the non-airborne approach, barreling out the door.

Once inside, we met two more of our hosts for the evening, Thomas and Will, Danielle and Dave's two beautiful young boys. Will was not yet one, and I guessed Thomas to be a few years his elder. The adults were enjoying pre-dinner conversation. I was fortunate enough to be invited into Thomas and Will's world of Legos. Their innocence, joy, and excitement were infectious. Our Lego party also included Tucker and Owen. I got the feeling that the two beautiful kids and those dogs were a package deal. Things could not be more perfect. I found myself immersed in the kind of energy that only young children and loving pets can provide.

One of the real benefits of a run like this is that you learn to appreciate the simple pleasures of life. It is so easy to come home at day's end, your dogs waiting, your family there, and a roof to provide comfort for sleep that evening. Do you take a moment to appreciate how lucky you are for any one of these things? I often times do not. It is so easy to become complacent. *It's just the way things are,* the subconscious mind says as we go about our business. These adventures bring everything so much more clearly into focus. It makes one aware of the beauty in all things. The dining room conversation was like a great symphony. I found myself just soaking up the voices, not so much what they were saying but rather the beauty and uniqueness of the sound.

I loved this space I was in. I felt gratitude for everything. I was aware, alert, conscious, and awake. There was an unlimited number of things to be appreciative of. I reflected for a moment, hopeful I could remain in this space after the run was over. I made myself a promise to always look for what was good in everyday. I was not the best house guest. I didn't participate in the conversations much, other than to answer a few questions. I probably appeared quite out of it. In some ways I was, and in others I was deeply in it.

I excused myself early, the allure of a real bed and tomorrow's daunting forecast of 100 degrees made that an easy choice. Everyone was in good spirits, and I was happy to know the socializing would continue into the night. Little did I know that as I drifted off to sleep my dear friend, Sara Laugh, was driving hundreds of miles from Iowa to surprise me. My lights were out before I hit the pillow.

Day 35

Laughy

Apparently, Sara had been planning her visit for quite some time. I can only imagine that these covert operations provided Jarred joy in contrast to his constant care-taking responsibilities. I was a bit more groggy than usual that morning. Indoor plumbing, showers, and a real bed may have signaled to the mind that the adventure was over, and now it could rest. Forever. It made starting the day even more challenging. It was a trade that had been well worth it, but I was most definitely in a fog as I exited the house for the RV.

"WHAT THE HELL YA DOING YA DUMB FU#$%R?!" she yelled from the curb, nearly giving me a heart attack. Up to that point, jumping into Lake Michigan's frigid waters had been the only thing that had provided a comparable shock to the system. Sara Laugh was not her real name. The Sara part yes, the laugh part had been earned. "Laughy," as she was known to friends, had a one of a kind, booming laugh that just by its nature, made others laugh. She had driven all the way from Iowa, arriving sometime after I had passed out cold. Her greeting shocked me out of my sleep-induced haze. I thought to myself, *How the...? What the...? Did you guys all know?* Looking around it was clear that everyone, indeed, did know. The morning went from zero to sixty just like that. Laughy was in the house! The day would be no match for this team.

It was cool and slightly overcast. The lake was an even deeper shade of beautiful this morning. The Michigan side of Lake Michigan had turned out to be a wonderful surprise. My naïveté had led me to believe that this side would be dumpy for some reason. I had never spent any time in Michigan, so naturally I just assumed it would all be rough and industrial. Of course, the whole state would be like Detroit, right? I've never been to Detroit either so it's entirely possible that assumption may also be incorrect. I could not have been more wrong. From north to south, the eastern side of Lake Michigan was spectacular. There are numerous small towns— St. Ignace in the UP, Petoskey, Traverse City, Arcadia, Manistee, Ludington—that come alive during the summer, each with its own flavor. Whether by car, bike or even foot, if you ever choose a trip up or down the coast of this Great Lake on the Michigan side, you will be glad you did.

The water also had its own unique qualities. It seemed hard to imagine that the same lake could look so different. The deepest of blues would melt into shades of green, brown in the shallows, and almost purple in other spots. It was dazzling, magnificent. On this day, as I left the RV to begin the day's run, it was as if Mother Nature was blowing me the coolest, sweetest of kisses from somewhere too far from shore to see. I spent a few moments facing out towards her sweet embrace with eyes closed. I breathed in deeply and exhaled fully. I listened, completely present, and I made sure to say "thank you."

From that first day, five weeks before, I had prayed to the lake, asking for her blessing and that she see me safely back to Navy Pier. Her occasional evening thunderstorms had entertained and awed us. Her fresh waters healed my legs and cooled me so that I could eat. Today, after so many stifling hot days, she wrapped me up in her cool breezes. Her hug provided comfort at a time that was most needed. I wanted to be sure she heard my "thank you" before starting the day's journey. We were in this together. I was this far, in large part, because of her many gifts.

The plan was for Sara to drive her car ahead to the halfway point, hop in with Jarred, and return to support me. It was great knowing that Jarred would have company. He and Sara had also been friends for years. I can't imagine how good that must have been for him. The first few miles flew by, and the legs felt great. Running right next to the lake, it was still a bit overcast and cool. Finally, the weatherman had missed the mark. The day's forecasted heat had not yet arrived. It was a beautiful stretch. The road meandered through the woods and past the occasional lake house. With Jarred being gone for a bit longer than usual, I was on my own for an hour and was very much enjoying the solitude. I had loaded up with plenty of calories and an extra water bottle before Jarred and Sara left. It would be no problem to last until their return. Unfortunately, I had not thought to bring the RV toilet with me. The morning breakfast decided it needed to be heard from. *Now.* It's amazing how after going an hour seeing only one or two cars, each time I tried to steal a squat off the side of the road, car after car kept rolling by. It became clear that if this act was going to happen in peace, a slight off-route run was needed. I wasn't in any need of extra miles, but this was becoming an emergency situation. A quick left turn onto a logging road and *Eureka!* A Port-a-Potty stood where there was no earthly reason for there to be one. I thought to myself, "God really does love adventurers."

Eventually, the RV found its way back to me. Nearly halfway done for the day, we took time to just hang out and soak up the company. Laughy asked what the hell was taking me so long, letting me know any real runner would have been done by now. She was probably right about that. I let her know that my hour-long poop was the culprit. She didn't seem at all interested in the photographic evidence. Everyone was doing their best to get the last word, regardless of the subject matter. These were among the best moments of the run, hanging out with friends, with not a care in the world. We were as free as could be, chilling out next to the lake. There was still a chunk of running to do, so after about thirty minutes the RV cruised away, and our game of leap frog was back on. The remaining miles went by as easily as any on the entire run. The cool temps that day were a *big* reason for that. The great energy in the RV played an even bigger role.

That night, we shared dinner at a steak house in South Haven, Michigan. The meal provided a great setting for seemingly endless laughs. Many stories from years past were retold, all a bit grander than they really were. Laughy made sure to let our server know what we were up to. Everyone who joined us for the run took great pleasure in bragging up what was going on. All the attention and kind words were very humbling. Almost without fail, every person we'd meet would have their own cancer stories. A sister, brother, or close friend had been diagnosed. In some cases, the person we were speaking with had fought cancer and survived. We also heard stories of loved ones lost, which really sucked, but always reminded us of why we were really out here.

We asked the server if there was any possibility of staying there for the night. We had not yet found or decided upon a resting place for the evening. It was getting late, and the steak house parking lot seemed like a great idea. None of us wanted to drive around in the food coma that was coming on fast. The manager, once aware of what we were doing, was quick to oblige. They opened at noon the next day. As long as we were out of there well before that, we were good to go. We assured him we would be long gone by the time people started showing up for work the next day. Laughy splurged for dinner, covering the entire tab. It was nearly ten o'clock when we retired to the RV. I was good for a couple hugs, and then excused myself to the back of the RV to get some *ZZZs*. Jarred always kept a good whiskey around for special occasions, of which there had been many. Laughy was more the Bud Light type. There was no telling how long those two might be at it. Their voices were the perfect bedtime lullaby. I couldn't really hear the words being said, but there was a joy in their tones that put a smile on my face as I drifted off.

Day 36

If the RV's a rockin'...

Waking up on the right side of the bed was guaranteed with Laughy along. She needed no coffee to find her stride. "Get up, get up, ya sleepy heads. Get up, get up, get out of bed!" With that, the day was off to a rousing start. Laughy was the "spoon full of sugar" that let the medicine go down. Jarred whipped up a great breakfast; the half dozen eggs over easy, slab of bacon, peanut butter toast, and heaping pile of potatoes he dropped in front of me had no chance. There may have even been a dill pickle spear or two. I destroyed that plate of food! I washed it all down with a half gallon of chocolate milk. Calories would not be an issue today.

We knew, at some point, Paco would be showing up. Meeks was en route as well. Sara and the two of them in the same RV would be a circus certainly worthy of three rings. It was great to have those kind of things to look forward to. Paco is a unique cat: part skateboard punk, part death metal fan, part cyclist, part adventurer, and all around great dude. He had boxed up his bike, flown from Denver to Detroit, and had been biking through Michigan the past few days in his quest to intercept us. His plan was to hang with us a while, catch a ferry, cross the lake to see Iron Maiden in Wisconsin, stay with his family in Green Bay for a couple days, box up the bike, and fly home. Genius plan.

Laughy was kind enough to allow the morning feast to settle a bit before ordering the run to start. It was necessary to walk that first mile to warm up the legs, while at the same time ensuring the morning groceries stayed down. The legs felt strong as my pace quickened. Just a couple miles up the road, our two-person support crew caught sight of a bearded cyclist who seemed to be in search of something. By the time I reached the van, the party was already in full swing! I don't know if this crew would be best described as the *Three Amigos* or the *Three Stooges*. Paco decided immediately to throw down a couple miles with me in his styling slippers. I think it was his way to really be a part of the run. No lie, he ran with me for the next few miles in canvas slippers that our grandparents were sporting fifty years ago. It didn't seem the least bit odd if you knew Paco. I wasn't too hard to keep up with, even in slippers. We stopped often, took pictures, and then suddenly found ourselves at a dead end in the middle of a small but very fancy little subdivision that wasn't on the map. It was either turn back, which was not an option, or forge ahead. The signs clearly read "No Trespassing," "No Biking Pass Through," and "Cameras on Premises." We debated for all of about three seconds and decided to break a law or two. We joked that no one would prosecute a dude in slippers and a guy running around Lake Michigan raising money for cancer survivors.

Fortunately, our gamble that no one would prosecute was never put to the test. It was only a half mile of bush whacking, and we were back on route and up to the RV. It was well before noon, but for Paco, the running was done. He had completed his latest mission, which was to find me and grab a piece of the run. The Iron Maiden concert wasn't for another couple days. The Three Stooges were reunited, drinks began to flow, and I officially had the rockin'est support crew in history.

The miles passed with ease. It seemed that each time I approached the RV after a few miles, the music and laughter could be heard a bit farther away. Paco and Laughy were the perfect example of one plus one equaling seven. The energy in that RV was growing exponentially every couple miles. The beers certainly fanned the already hot flames of hilarity. Jarred had a sister and brother in arms; it must have seemed like an entirely different planet compared to the world he had existed in up to this point. No more was he sitting idly at the roadside for thirty minutes at a time, waiting for me to shuffle by, just so he could drive two more miles and do the same. Nope. He was the head honcho of the party bus now. The run provided all of us a chance to enjoy one hell of a time together.

Meeks eventually caught up to us as it was time to get Laughy on her way back home. She had driven her car to the steakhouse the previous night. Jarred and Paco were going to take her back while I carried on. Meeks would look after me in their absence. I'd later find out she drove until sleepiness forced her into a roadside catnap at 3 a.m. before she knocked out the remaining miles of her trip back to Des Moines. Her return trip home was well over 600 miles. That was evidence of a friend of the highest degree; I was blessed with many.

The twenty-six miles and change went by all too quickly that day.

Steven Cannon

I wished our running band of gypsies could have stayed together so much longer. It was one of very few days that I was a bit sad when the last mile was done. Had the day called for thirty or forty miles, I believe the legs would have delivered.

A hotel and a giant pizza feed were waiting for us. Meeks had set up both and directed us to our final stop for the day. Meeks and I would crash in the hotel, but Jarred and Paco had bigger plans. I didn't get the feeling that sleep played a prominent role in those plans. Certainly great stories would be forthcoming in the morning. After everyone took their turn soaking up a long hot shower, two large pizzas took a savage beating. It's entirely possible the cardboard boxes were devoured as well. I made quick work of a couple root beers and Meeks did the same with his diet Dews. Paco continued his day long domination of the "Oat sodas" while Jarred began introducing ice cubes to some of Kentucky's finest. The party was on. Paco and Jarred did their best to convince Meeks and me to stay up and raise a little hell for a while. I did accompany them back to the RV for a bit, but Meeks hung back to update the blog for those who looked forward to his nightly updates. As tempting as hanging out with these two hooligans was, I eventually excused myself to the hotel. *A man's gotta know his limits,* I thought to myself. I could hear their laughs and what sounded like Sinatra as I walked from the RV towards my home for the night. I'd be asleep shortly; they would not. All was just as it should be. I paused at the hotel door, breathed in deeply and exhaled the same. I couldn't see the lake, but I turned toward her and, again, silently said, "Thank you."

Day 37

Completely empty

Fighting bushes was not easy business. We found out that Paco had got into a nasty fist fight with a large bush and had enlisted Jarred's help. I'm sure it made perfect sense at three or four in the morning. They had headed out the night before on a leisurely bike ride, accompanied with an ample supply of Templeton Rye and Sinatra's greatest hits. Perhaps the bush had insulted one or even both. We all got a great laugh out of the story. Never getting to see the bush, I don't know who got the better of the altercation.

Hotel sleeps were the ultimate double-edged sword. Meeks and I had checked into the Comfort Inn the prior evening, made our way to the room, and promptly set the AC as low as it would go. He had been documenting each day's events for the blog and was our lifeline to the outside world. He accompanied us for a few days at the start and was fired up to rejoin the team for the homestretch. Brian, AKA Meeks, had been my college roommate. He was pretty much always pumped but now was at a level of pumped that was uncharted. We were quite the sight, sleeping in long sleeve shirts and stocking caps. It reminded me of a man starving for water after days in the desert. Once lucky enough to find water, it is not wise to guzzle. However, the temptation is impossible to resist. The AC was no different. Each day had been so brutally hot. We had some respite in the RV, but it was impossible to get the rig really chilled.

The problem with dropping the room temperature to sixty degrees or less is that the body *really* shuts down. It feasts on the cool temps, convincing itself that the torture is over. Many years prior, while bike touring from Colorado to Iowa to meet up with RAGBRAI, I had encountered the same issue for the first time. Mighty (AKA Keri Mounce) and I had decided after a few days of fighting 100-degree-plus temperatures through Colorado and western Nebraska, that we would treat ourselves to a hotel sleep. It had been nearly impossible to drag ourselves out into the already sweltering day the next morning. We had to make a vow of silence for the first few hours because we were so fouled out. It was either silence or a fist fight. Mighty is all of 120 pounds, but in her mood, attempting conversation would have been the equivalent of sticking my head into a bag of cats. Silence seemed a better plan.

The savior that morning for Meeks and me was that sleeping in was not an option; we had an interview at 7:30 a.m. with Chicago television station WCIU that had been covering us for weeks before the run. The *You and Me This Morning* crew had been real friends to the run.

Everyone had been doing a great job not speaking of the finish, but we all could feel it coming. I was within 100 miles. I could almost taste the end. The energy was palpable, so much so that it frightened me if I thought about it. I realized, as we prepared for the interview, that I never consciously thought I *wouldn't* make it. I also realized that there was a part of me, hidden deep away, that never thought I *would* make it.

One of the great blessings of the run was that it brought people together. Old friends I had not kept in touch with came out of nowhere to support the run, some of them traveling great distances to be a part of it. Many others donated, some $1,000 or more. It was not only humbling but also reassuring. The texts, voice mails, and emails were pouring in:

"You're home free, man"
"Just a few days to go"
"Unbelievable"
"You did it!!"

Every day, the news is filled with *bad this* or *negative that*. It's how they sell their product. I had not seen a TV, radio or computer screen for weeks because I had been immersed in the run. Instead, I woke every day to kind words and messages of support. Donations kept pouring in. The world is not always what the news or Internet portrays. It is full of love. People are caring, supportive and enjoy a good adventure.

We finished the interview via Skype. Meeks would be handling support for the first part of the day. Jarred was going to take care of chores: mail, laundry, and maybe a little R and R. Paco's journey would be taking him away from us today. He had a death metal concert to get to. His ferry was waiting fifty-five miles away to take him across the lake to Milwaukee. It was hard to watch him roll away. He, like all who had visited, had been a huge shot in the arm for all of us.

South Haven, Michigan had been good to us, and like so many towns before, it would have been a lovely place to kick it for a day or two, but we had to push on. I forced down a bite of muffin and poured as much chocolate milk in me as I could hold. The heat index was well into the nineties and was predicted to top 100 degrees, *again*.

The two-lane highway offered a nice shoulder for running. It did not, however, offer any relief from the sun. The double whammy was in full effect. The sun was like a hand that continually attempted to push me down into the asphalt. As brutal as the heat was from above, it was the asphalt below my feet that multiplied the sun's effects. Whatever the temperature, it was at least twenty degrees higher coming up from the black tar. By mile four it was already time for a change of clothes. Everything was completely soaked in sweat. Imagine what that laundry bag was like for Jarred.

We joked about me being like Celine Dion with all the wardrobe changes. Dry socks, shorts, and shirt were all put on for the next *set*. We would fill the bandana with ice and roll it up to put around my neck. I didn't want any mileage updates. I'd disappear deep into the stillness. No energy wasted: not on thoughts, needless conversation, nothing. Eventually a town appeared on the horizon, and soon Jarred would let me know that I was done. Unfortunately, on this day, it was my body that delivered the message I was done.

The slight incline seemed like a mountain as I shuffled my way up the bridge separating Benton Harbor and St. Joseph, Michigan. Benton Harbor, it turns out, is the world headquarters of Whirlpool. On the other side, the RV waited. The last few minutes had wasted me, the toll of the past thirty-seven days and over twenty miles in the oven today came crashing down.

I was barely able to step into the RV and crumpled into the couch. I asked the question I never allowed myself to ask. "How much farther, Jarred?" The only acceptable answer to my broken body and mind would have been, "No farther, you're done." That, I knew, would not be the answer. Jarred could see I was in trouble. It had come so fast. At the last stop, although challenged, all systems were still functioning. That was no longer true.

"Almost, buddy. Take a right off the highway up ahead, and you are home free." He was lying, I would soon find out, but he knew after so many days that I could not handle the truth just then. He was correct. I couldn't find the energy even to speak. Nothing was left. I was in pure survival mode. All systems shut down except the one that would allow my legs to keep moving. I stepped out of the RV and tried to shuffle forward somehow. My head facing the ground, I was too tired to lift it. I vaguely remember thinking that this was the place. This was the rare place when one has truly given their all. I had come to Lake Michigan for many reasons. One was to find my limit. I wanted to know what waited for me when seemingly, nothing was left.

I had reached the end of the highway. I was not, "home free," as Jarred had promised. "Just to the end of that parking lot, at the end of that path," he told me. There was no anger in me. There was no energy for that. I also knew he had been right to lie to me. Meeks and Jarred decided to accompany me for the last push.

It would be one of my favorite memories of the run. Meeks on one side of me, Jarred on the other. They watched over me, making sure I didn't fall, as I could no longer shuffle safely on my own.

Steven Cannon

I could barely even walk. It was the three of us now. It was our run. Their words kept me moving those last few hundred yards. I sobbed as we finished the day, completely empty, and so grateful for the love and support these two had given me. I put my arms over each of their shoulders, unable to carry my own weight any longer. We turned around to make the walk back to the RV. Not a single word was spoken.

Once back in the RV, the process of recovery began immediately. The physical goal was always the same, even after thirty-seven days: attempt every day to be as close as possible to the level I was the day before. This meant that I tried never to push too hard or let the tank get too empty. My body was under tremendous strain. I had done my best to control the effort, but somehow the tank had become as close to empty as I could ever remember. Recovery drinks were ready and chilled which helped in two ways. Replenishing my fluids was key. The cold drinks also helped to lower my core temperature which in turn would stimulate my appetite.

If ever I needed extra TLC, that was the night. Fortunately for all of us, we were headed for exactly that. A dear friend from high school, Lisa Rechkemmer, now a podiatrist near Chicago, had a lake house not far away. She, like so many others who supported us, was excited to offer up her home. She would not be there but had no problem opening her place to us. The short drive allowed my body time to recover slightly. Once in the driveway, our finely tuned team went to work. I headed straight for the shower. Cold showers were not enjoyable but sometimes were necessary. When possible I'd sit in Lake Michigan's frigid waters at the end of the day to cool down and help reduce the swelling in my legs. If not possible, the coldest shower I could handle would take its place. I went

FORTY DAYS

straight to bed after the shower. Exhausted still, I set the alarm for 7 pm. There was no need to instruct Jarred. I knew, that by the time I woke, laundry would be in the works, and a kick-ass meal would be waiting. Again, there was no way to adequately convey to our host how much we had needed her home that night and how grateful we were for her kindness and generosity. I passed out immediately, as I sank into that wonderful bed.

Day 38

Michigan, thank you.

The recovery drinks, the healing cold shower, pre-dinner nap, and the feast Jarred made, led to an incredible night's sleep. Most nights were spent repositioning every hour or so. My body was always on alert, always hot. There was a never-ending search for a non-sweat-soaked area of the sheets. Even in the air conditioned RV or the occasional real bed, my body never completely cooled. Surprisingly, I got up early. I was ready to run; couldn't wait! I felt great physically and mentally. It was crazy thinking that just twelve hours ago, I had pretty much been a dead man walking.

Our starting point for the day was to be about a half hour away. It was an easy decision to make. There was no way I was going to wake up Jarred or Meeks, both sleeping soundly. I'd start my running from Lisa's front door and, whenever they awoke, had their coffee, breakfast and were ready to go, we'd figure out the rest of the day based on how many miles I got in that morning. It felt like

FORTY DAYS

a very small way for me to return some TLC to them.

Lisa's cottage was magical. The interior was stunning in a way that one usually expects to find only in magazines. Brazilian cherry hardwood floors, white cabinets, stainless appliances—it was perfectly decorated down to the last detail and made one feel immediately at home. It was the sort of house where one could spend years curled up with nothing but an iPad, keyboard, and a healthy imagination, and bang out novel after novel. I loved the idea of Jarred and Brian waking up in that comfort. I left a note explaining that I was out on the run and would return a bit later. Day Thirty-eight was going to be brutally hot. The weatherman said so, weather.com agreed, and their forecasts gave no indication that there would be any break in the heat coming.

I walked at first, maybe for a mile. Then I began to jog, barely faster than the walk. Random thoughts raced through my brain. This was not new territory. The difference was, defusing the bomb was getting easier. I began to observe my thoughts with no judgment at all. When I did this, the thoughts started to slow. As they faded, I tried to become my breathing as I had learned to do on earlier runs.

I loved the comparison of the mind being like an ocean: wild and uncontrollable at the surface, but as you explore beneath the surface, the deeper you travel, the more peaceful and calm it is. This run was no longer a physical journey; it had become a much deeper spiritual experience.

Lisa's cottage was on a tiny lake, and this was the setting for my morning run. Two miles into the day, Mother Nature came calling, or more accurately, screaming. Apparently, Jarred's feast from the night before was ready to be out of me. If I continued, it would be

190

five more miles before getting back to Lisa's. Turning back seemed like the best option, but that would break the steadfast rule. Never back track. There were no random Port-a-Potties to save me this time. I was running out of time in a hurry.

Fortunately, just before having to squat on the side of the road and hope for the best, a third option presented itself. The local golf course was just ahead, and it looked like the clubhouse was open. I went in and asked to use the facilities. It wouldn't have mattered the answer. The stunning woman behind the counter pointed the way, and with great relief, the traumatic situation was resolved.

It seemed rude to quickly duck in and duck out. Had the fan in the bathroom not been working, I probably would have done that very thing. I took a moment to express my thanks, explained what I was doing and had a nice chat with the woman. The people in Michigan were always very friendly. I said goodbye and continued on the morning run.

By the time I returned to Lisa's, Jarred and Meeks were up and at 'em. Getting seven miles in before it became crazy hot had been a solid plan. It allowed me to take a nice chunk out of the day, and I could see that my crew was refreshed and in great spirits. Feeling pretty good, I decided to do another lap while Jarred got the RV ready for the day. Meeks was again pumped and decided to run along for a little bit. It would be great to have him along. We walked for awhile and talked about the day. It was already feeling pretty warm, but the sunshine and fresh air had Meeks all fired up. We picked up the pace a little, telling stories and talking as we moved along. I could feel his excitement. I fed off of it.

When we got to the clubhouse, I suggested Meeks turn back because he'd have to cover two more miles on the return trip. He didn't want to, but I also didn't want him to get in trouble. The temps were rising fast, and four miles of running would be four miles more than he had run in quite some time, maybe ever. I asked if he would bring me another bottle of the Hammer Heed drink mix when he got back to the cabin. This gave him a good reason to turn back and made his return jog more of a quest than backtracking. Upon returning to the house, Meeks would grab another bottle of fluids, hop in his truck, and come find me.

Meeks did so, in good time, and traded the full bottle for my empty, then zipped ahead in his truck before parking. Apparently, he had a bit of the running fever. I could see him in the distance running back to meet me. It was so cool to see his excitement and the joy he was finding through running. The temperature was now approaching a million degrees, give or take, and when we got back to his truck, I still had about two miles to go. I thought I might need another bottle and really didn't want my new running partner to die on me in this heat. He was kind enough, or smart enough to agree and rushed back to the cottage in the truck to grab one more bottle.

The second seven-mile jaunt had been much tougher than the first, but it meant I was over halfway done for the day. I would take time to eat, shower, power nap, and then tackle the remaining twelve-plus miles. Meeks decided that he was done running for the day and decided to strike out in search of a much needed haircut. He was then going to continue on to Michiana Shores, Indiana, to find a couple rooms for the night.

The fourteen miles I ran with Meeks that morning bought Jarred some well-deserved rest and plenty of time to get everything in the RV spruced up and ready to go for the remaining two and a half

Steven Cannon

days. The work Jarred did on a daily basis was astounding. I have often said I understand on some level how I was able to run around Lake Michigan. I thought again how I did not understand how Jarred did what he did. Everyday without fail, he cooked for me, filled every drink bottle, did all of the laundry, dealt with my mood swings, and drove that RV a couple miles at a time for forty days straight and 1,037 miles.

From the outset that day, we were home free. We had traveled thirty-seven days and totaled well over 900 miles. Each day was an awesome challenge, and there were still many miles to go. It was clear that our stay at Lisa's had done wonders for all of us. On Day Fourteen we had crossed into Michigan from Wisconsin. We had been in Michigan for twenty-three days. Today, we would leave Michigan and cross into Indiana.

Crossing a state line was a big deal, a really big deal. Indiana meant that we had only one more state line to cross: Illinois. Michiana Shores, Indiana was our Day Thirty-eight destination. Despite my early jaunts, the remaining twelve miles of the day were incredibly challenging. There had been days when we were able to run right on the lake, and her breezes would provide relief from the stifling heat. Today was not one of those days. The past few days had been hot, but just normal hot—meaning in the low nineties. Mother Nature was going to make sure we earned every mile of these last two and a half days.

Running away from the lake meant there was no breeze and no hopping in the water when things got too hot. By the middle of the afternoon, the temperature was well into the nineties, which easily pushed the thermometer into the hundred-plus mark on the road. The route was pretty flat heading into Michiana, and we found a

FORTY DAYS

frontage road that got us off the busy highway shoulder. I had long ago lost the fear of cars buzzing close past me. It was just a part of the job. Looking back, it was probably a bit reckless, but thousands of cars passed within feet of me on the run everyday without incident.

For some time now, I had been able to turn my mind off almost at will. I could go into meditative states that would only be interrupted by Jarred and the support vehicle on the side of the road. Occasionally I would not even notice them. Music too had become a thing of the past. I had become a part of a different world, one without TV or email, text messages or newspapers. My world was that road, and I immersed myself in it. Music was just another manufactured noise that my mind no longer needed or would even tolerate. I existed in the simplest of places. My mind had been replaced or demoted by my soul. The sound of my breath, my footsteps, and the lake became a lullaby. I had run out of my mind. Time and distance had lost most of their meaning and hold on me.

The frontage road ran alongside a set of railroad tracks which were bordered on both sides by a very inviting level dirt path. Of course, it was illegal to run on since it was an active Amtrak railway. The frontage road was asphalt and cooking me from the ground up. It was not a tough choice. It was nearing the end of the work day, and the Amtrak trains would be coming by from time to time. The conductors of those things are annoyingly thorough on blaring their horns, so I was not too worried about being knocked out of my zen state by an oncoming train running me over. After thirty-eight days, it all seemed perfectly sensible.

As I approached Michiana Shores, I could see a giant sign in the distance. Signs of this size were reserved for state borders. I was about to put the state of Michigan in my rear view mirror. We had been a guest for over three weeks, starting on the east side of the great lake, hundreds of miles ago. I made it a ritual to take a picture of each state line sign with the LIVESTRONG bracelet on my wrist. I'd have to jump the tracks and slog through the roadside ditch to get close enough, but it would be well worth the effort. With a touch of the iPhone camera button, I entered Indiana. I was one state closer to completing my journey.

I didn't know it at the time, but two of my closest friends, Mike and Keri Wallace, were en route from Iowa to surprise me. Jarred and I stuck to our guns. There was no discussing Day Forty until Day Forty, but there was no denying how close we were. Day Thirty-eight was done. Nearly.

I'm not sure what time it was when the knock on the hotel door came. I knew by now that Mike and Keri were on their way. It didn't matter how tired I was; I popped up and shuffled my way to the door. I was decked out in my recovery tights, stocking cap and Strassburg socks, designed to keep the tendons in my feet stretched while I slept; the twenty-six miles a day had done little to heal the plantar fasciitis I had developed in both my feet during training. I must have been quite a sight when I opened the door for Mike and Keri. The cavalry had arrived.

Mike's quote on our blog early in the run had often served as my rallying cry. "Steve is a warrior. He has been running everyday for over five months to train. He knows the run is possible. Even probable. He is in his element. There is no place he would rather be. He will be standing on the Navy Pier in thirty-seven days as scheduled. There is no doubt. I *know* he can do it." The energy they brought would more than make up for the sleep I'd lose. Wally and Mighty

FORTY DAYS

(as they are better known) were all smiles, and the hugs we shared felt so good. They had lots of questions. I shared stories with them about the past few weeks, and we laughed and talked for an hour. It was now Day Thirty-nine, 1 a.m. I went back to sleep. *Almost there,* I thought. *You're almost there.*

Day 39

The homestretch

The day began just like the thirty-eight others that had preceded it. I woke up and sat at the side of the bed. I did this for two reasons. One was to let my mind clear a bit. Time and place, except for state borders, had lost their meaning for me long ago. I'd take a few minutes here each morning to sort of calibrate. Where I was, what day it was, and things like that. The other reason was purely physical. If I just hopped right out of bed I'd likely snap the plantar tendons in both feet. Plantar fasciitis had been with me for the entire run, and we had reached an agreement long ago. I would sit at the edge of the bed for a few minutes, letting the blood start to feed my feet, and in exchange my ligaments agreed to let go of their hold on my feet shortly afterward.

Spirits were high as we packed our new crew into the support vehicle. Tobin had also rejoined the squad, which meant bike support would be with us all day. This would become a real bonus as the temps soared later in the day. My mind, which had been run to sleep for the past few weeks, was now wide awake and had plenty to say. *Don't blow it now. Those feet are gonna pop! How embarrassing if you got this close and had to quit.* Wally and Mighty were just what I needed: a pacifier for my mind.

I met Wally about fifteen years earlier. Wally was part of the legendary, larger-than-life RAGBRAI bike team known as Team Bad Boy. Wally rode a bike with a 100 gallon cooler on the back of it. The other rigs consisted of a 55-gallon steel drum made into a smoker (which I now ride), a full wet bar, a home stereo with generator, and yes, even the kitchen sink. The sink was rigged with a bilge pump that would let you turn on the spigot and pour yourself a margarita. The combined weights of these bikes was around 800 pounds, and they rode them everywhere, including the toughest mountain passes in Colorado during many Ride the Rockies tours.

Mighty and Wally have been married for years and are a great fit. Mighty is 190 pounds of crazy crammed into a 5'2, 120 pound body, which is why we call her 'the mighty' and why she at times gets herself in trouble. She often forgets she's not the 190 pounder. Mighty and I have adventure-raced, marathoned, and raised hell all over the country. Many of the best adventures of my life are because of and have been shared with these two. Day Thirty-nine was a huge day. I knew, and my mind knew, that I'd crawl hands and knees into Chicago on Day Forty if need be.

We left the hotel around 9 a.m., and the temps were in the eighties and climbing fast. Nearly the entire day would be spent on trails along the southern tip of Lake Michigan. Jarred would not have access to us at all times, so Tobin keeping us supplied with liquids was key.

Steven Cannon

The south portion of Lake Michigan was home to the Indiana Dunes. This was where the idea for The Run to Cure Cancer had come to me to me over a year ago. It was surreal to think that I would be running past that very place on this day.

Day Thirty-nine also meant that I would see my family. A couple months earlier, it had been decided that if I were to make it this far, we would end the day by driving into Chicago and staying at the same hotel where we had started. My mom and my sister would be there waiting for me.

Although it had been well over a year since I'd visited Indiana Dunes, I remembered the trail well: crushed limestone and flat as a pancake. There was no tree cover on the trail, and *Mom* was blocked from view by the woods, which meant no breeze. It would become one of the hottest days of the entire run. I craved all of the intensity that the run and Mother Nature could give.

We started by making a video dedication to cancer fighters everywhere. Donations had really picked up as we closed in on the finish. I was hopeful that these last two days would get us over the $30,000 mark. The first couple miles passed slowly, as the body started to warm to the task. Time passed quickly though, as there was plenty of conversation. I shared more stories about the last thirty-eight days. By the time Jarred met us, around the five mile mark, we were already soaked. I don't know what the temperature was, but the fact that it already felt the way it did at only 10 a.m. meant we were in for a test.

Jarred had everything ready as always. Drinks and watermelon were shared among us all. We couldn't hang out too long—comfort was dangerous—but stayed just long enough to drop the core temps and get back on the trail. Behind the scenes there was much going on that I was unaware of. As we shuffled down the nearly deserted trail, I got my first surprise of the day. Another runner was headed our way. As he got a bit closer, I could tell he was okay despite the heat. He had the look. Even from a distance, I sensed this guy was a runner. I was looking forward to giving him a high five for being a badass and obviously choosing to run in this inferno.

He was a runner, a genuine badass, and my friend Scott Mills. I hadn't seen him in person since before leaving Des Moines for the run, but I saw him everyday inside the RV. His picture was taped up next to all the other cancer fighters we were running for. I met Scott a year earlier. There was a cool group of trail runners back home, and that's how we had initially run into each other. I was drawn to the guy's spirit straight away. He loved the outdoors, loved running, and embraced the adventure of seeing "how far." There was a going away party for me just days before I left. Scott showed up to wish me luck and also to let me know he had been diagnosed with lymphoma that day.

I couldn't believe he was here! I mean I could, but I couldn't. He was in the middle of treatment, but you would never have known it. He was strong and upbeat and classic Scott, loving the intensity of the day. I was so happy. I felt so loved. I was giving all I had physically and emotionally to get around that lake, but I was getting so much more back. Each day, I received many messages from friends, family, and people I had never met. Every person, every moment added new meaning for me. The very people the run was for, people like Scott, had taught me how important the many gifts of life were because they can be taken from us in an instant.

We had ourselves a nice caravan forming now. *Damn, it was hot.* I don't think any of us would have changed it though. We all knew that the intensity of the conditions would only make the stories sweeter. After ninety minutes on the trail, Wally headed back to the previous night's hotel to get their car, and Scott went off with his family to enjoy the rest of their Fourth of July weekend. Mighty and Tobin would soldier on for another hour. The heat was stifling. Ice was packed into bandanas, rolled up, and tied around our necks. It would only take a mile for it to melt. Every pore opened up and fluid went out nearly as quickly as it went in. It was dangerously hot. Heat exhaustion or heat stroke was just one stupid move away. I couldn't wait to get to that hotel for the night. Air conditioning and a real bed would be so sweet. Out there on the trail however, it was one step, one mile at a time. Survival mode.

It was time for Mighty to call it a day. She could have continued, but she and Wally were headed back to Chicago where we would meet them later at the hotel. Back in the RV we all shared a big hug, and I told them we'd see 'em soon. Tobin and Jarred worked together to make sure I'd have enough fluids for the last stretch. I carried two bottles of Hammer's Heed and Tobin put two more on his bike. We had less than six miles to go. I tied up one last ice bandana and bailed out of the AC-filled RV. We came upon a small covered bridge on the trail after three or four miles. As I sat on the bench seat with my head hung low, the sweat poured out of me. I don't believe I have ever been so hot, so tired, and still so at peace. I don't remember if I even had a thought, but it was a feeling, a serenity I'll never forget.

As I got up, music was blasting in my ears, and my body was flush with adrenaline. I knew the day's run was nearly over. There had only been a few times during the run that I let go and allowed myself to run all out, for fear of injury. On Day Thirteen that was exactly what had happened. It nearly derailed me. That day was a distant memory. There was not a sore or tight spot anywhere in me. I allowed my pace to quicken and my stride to go. If you are a runner you know this space. It is that last half mile of your first 5k or 10k. It is that last mile of your first marathon, when only an hour before you wondered how you could possibly finish. Yet there you were, running full out. Unstoppable! The end of the trail was in sight, and the RV would be just around the corner. I wished for the trail to go on forever so the feeling would last. My legs began to slow, and the last few steps were done. I hugged Tobin with tears of joy streaming down my face. The run had come over 1,000 miles. It was time to go to Chicago.

Jarred, Tobin, and I loaded our sweaty carcasses into the RV. It was surreal to be headed back into Chicago. The run had been punishing. The temperature had gone easily past the hundred degree mark. It didn't matter now. The beating the day had given me was already practically forgotten.

I knew my mom and sister were waiting at the hotel. There had been moments during the last few days when I would think about what that meeting would be like. Each time, I would have to cut the thoughts short. The run had opened me up so much. I was raw, and just the thought of seeing them, hugging them, would start me sobbing. Every single day started with a message from my mom. She had been through so much. The run had her worrying every day. Uncle Mike, her brother, had died just a week earlier. Yet, she never wavered. She was my hero. My sister, Kristan, and I spoke and texted every day as well. The two of them have always meant the world to me, but the run had taught me, even more, how valuable all our relationships are. It was okay now, I could let everything go. I didn't have to hold anything inside.

Meeks had secured a great parking spot close to the Hilton, which was no small task for an RV in downtown Chicago. Jarred, as usual, rolled that RV right into Chicago like he owned the place. I imagine he was pretty excited for some new humans to talk to and a real bed as well. He deserved that and much more. Meeks guided us into our spot, almost exactly the same place we had parked forty days earlier. Crazy. Tobin and Jarred rolled right out of the door. I was a bit slower. What I lacked in speed, I made up for in happiness. As we walked towards and then past the valet parking, I was trying to see through the revolving doors to find my mom. Where was she? I couldn't wait to hug her so she knew everything was okay, so she knew that I was here for *her* now. The revolving doors swung me into the crisp, cool hotel, and everything became this incredible blur. Mom, Sis, and I were in each other's arms, laughing, crying, hugging, hugging, hugging. Nothing else existed at that moment. I was oblivious to anything outside that three-person circle.

I knew some friends, including Wally and Mighty, were in the hotel bar, so eventually we started heading that way. It had been nearly twenty years since I had last seen Kyle Beaird. He had been a good friend during my Iowa City years, and the run had put us back in touch. After hearing of Uncle Mike's death, he had offered, unsolicited, to drive me back home, wait, and return me safely back to the run. I'll never forget that. Tim Kelly was another great friend from my days in Iowa City. He had brought his family to join the party and see the sights. Trent Smith and I had been roommates back in the day. He and his wife Kelli were there, along with their two awesome kids. They had made the trip all the way from

FORTY DAYS

Des Moines. It was hard to be disappointed about anything at that moment, but I wished my niece, Alyssa could have made the trip. It would have been cool had she been able to share this moment. She may have been the biggest fan of the run and saw me through some pretty rough patches. *Bang!* She popped out from around the corner. Things seemed perfect now. It seemed everyone was there. We all continued toward the bar, and there they were: Aunt Patty and her brother Eddie. The fact that they had come so far to be here, so soon after Uncle Mike's death, nearly dropped me. When our eyes met, I just stopped, unable to say or do anything. How do you accept that kindness, and so much love? I couldn't say anything. I heard them saying how proud they were of me, and that Uncle Mike was proud of me too. We just held each other. It felt like my heart might pop. I had so much love for all these people, and here they all were for me. There would end up being more surprises in the bar, more friends who made the trip. It was an extraordinary evening. We all sat together, sharing stories, and eating. A lot!

Occasionally, I would take a deep breath and just be. I was doing everything I could to burn the moments into my soul. If anything could be perfect, this was it. The party would continue for a few more hours, but it was time for me to head for bed. We'd have to drive out of Chicago early in the morning to take down Day Forty. It was forecast to be another scorching day. We all shared a final *big* hug. Alyssa signed up for helping her creaky *funcle* get to his room and making sure he didn't sleep through his alarm. It would be bad form to miss Day Forty after all. She and I talked for an hour, much like we had so many nights earlier. I thought that today may be as good as it ever gets. I'd never felt more blessed, more loved.

Day 40

Home

Donations had poured in the past few days pushing us well over the $30,000 mark. We were all very proud of the amount and incredibly grateful to all that had played any part in getting us there. The back of the RV was covered with words of inspiration and thanks from those we had met along the way. All was perfect! Forty days earlier, we had left Navy Pier and headed north. There was only one thing we all had known with certainty on that day. It was hot. Blazing hot. The hottest Memorial Day in the history of Chicago hot! Forty days later, Mother Nature had her furnace turned up full blast once again. She was definitely *not* the Windy City today. There was no breeze to bring relief from the lake's cool water. Chicago would welcome us home just as she had sent us away.

We loaded into the RV and headed south from the hotel. Steve Falck, Tobin, and Jarred were all with me for the final day. Tobin had been there at the start, and it was great to have him here at the

FORTY DAYS

end. Steve Falck is a lobbyist back home in Des Moines. I would later realize that perhaps, lifetimes prior, he had gotten his start as a town crier. He had his shoes laced up and would be at my side for the entire day's run back to Navy Pier. It was no small task considering the conditions, but he was an accomplished marathoner. I doubt either of them had a full understanding of what it meant to have them be a part of this day. No matter where life took us from that day forward, this journey, this run, would always bind us.

Their voices started to drift away as my mind wandered back to Indiana Dunes. Two years earlier, at a friend's suggestion, I had headed there for a run. That run inspired a question. *I wonder if anyone has ever run around this big sucker?* The answer, it turned out, was "No."

Every day of the run I asked for the mighty lake's blessing and each evening thanked her for delivering me safely. Lake Michigan was a part of me now. I felt myself on the verge of tears. Disbelief, gratitude, love, sadness, and joy all welled up just below the surface. I don't know if I had ever believed this day would come. It wasn't a thought or conversation that was allowed, with myself or others. The twists and turns of my time here on earth had somehow delivered me to this place. Was it luck? I had made so many bad choices early in life. I could have easily ended up dead or in jail. Maybe all of these journeys were somehow a penance, an attempt to make right on so many wrongs. If not luck, perhaps some divine force delivered me through the dark times. I hoped to be repaying that faith. There was also a debt to be paid. It is a debt we all carry. I had been given this gift of life. It is repaid by living it to the fullest. It has been said that we all get to contribute a verse to life. What will your verse be?

Steven Cannon

"You ready man?!"

I'm not sure if Falck or Tobin had asked the question or if it was the first or third attempt to get my attention. We had reached our starting point. I looked at both of them, took a deep breath, and nodded.

Tobin swung the RV door open to get his bike out. The cool, crisp air inside the RV quickly disappeared. Falck and I exchanged a glance that said, "Holy shit, it's hot!" We followed Tobin and his bike out of the RV. Jarred joined us. A few words were shared; hugs all around. We had done it. Heat be damned. We had done it. It was time for a six hour victory lap.

It took only minutes until all of us, Tobin included, were drenched. We were fortunate that our paved trail was tree-lined on both sides. It kept the morning sun, still low in the sky, from really putting us under stress. What the sun missed, though, the humidity made up for. Tobin had the bike loaded with drinks. Falck and I both had our hand-held bottles. As we got closer to the Windy City, it would become more difficult for Jarred to get to us. There would not be the usual game of "see you in a mile or so" leap frog.

The early miles passed easily. We joked and we chatted about this and that. We could have easily just been friends out for a casual day of running and biking. Sure it was hot, but it had been hot most days, and this was certainly not most days, it was *the* day. Everything was lighter, easier. The alarm had been a welcome sound that morning. The truth was, I was already awake when it went off. I was a young boy, just waiting for someone to give me the okay to go downstairs to unwrap Christmas presents. I couldn't wait to start running. That dreaded walk to the toilet to take a pee was somehow shorter and less painful. For the past thirty-nine days, the thought of twenty-six miles was not allowed early in the morning. It would render me helpless. That morning it was so very welcome. It energized me to the fullest.

We eventually exited the path and found ourselves running the streets of South Chicago. There's a pretty fair amount of asphalt in Chicago and no shortage of streets. It was one giant rock, baking in the sun. No longer were we free from Mother Nature's blazing gaze. The lake sat quietly. She offered no cooling breezes that day. Tobin and Jarred collaborated to keep us hydrated. As excited as we were to be on the home stretch, we still had to be smart. The weatherman warned of the dangers of even being outside. He certainly would not have recommended throwing down six hours of running. I'm sure there were more than a few heat-related problems in local emergency rooms that day. We were not going to be adding to the numbers.

It was surreal, running through the Chicago city streets and over the old metal bridges. Falck didn't miss a single opportunity to tell people what we were doing. If we ran within a block of somebody, he was gonna tug on their ear a bit. People really got into it. A shout of encouragement, a thumbs up, a "Way to go man!" or a high five were the usual results of Falck's PR.

However, while drinking and soaking our caps from one of the many fountains along the lake shore, we had a more meaningful encounter. I will forever remember her hug. Falck had shared what we were doing with a guy and his wife as I tried to do everything short of climb into the drinking fountain. The woman was a cancer survivor out for a walk. She apologized many times for not having any money to give. Her husband took quite a few pictures, and I was the recipient of many love filled hugs. "People like you save lives. Saved my life. Thank you. I love you," she said to me as we hugged one last time. Now, you can believe in chance if you like. I don't. I had run over 1,000 miles, and by "chance," on the final leg of the run, at that very moment, this woman happens to be at this fountain? Seeing the two of them, so in love and grateful to be out together on this day, was a blessing. I'd like to think we all left the encounter better for it. I know I did.

It was so damned hot, we stopped running on the black asphalt trail. We ran on the grass shoulders instead. Tobin rolled up and showed us his bike computer. It read 112 degrees. We all knew it wasn't quite that hot, but we got a kick out if it. Shuffling along and staring just a few feet ahead had become habit hundreds of miles ago. Falck chatted. Some things I heard, others I did not. At times I was totally present, while at others my mind drifted, recounting people and events from days past. I can't be sure how long it had been in view, but as I looked up from my focal point just ahead of me I could see it clearly.

Even miles away, it was unmistakable. The sight of it over-whelmed me to tears. There was a sudden realization that we had really done it. The visual proof was there. Navy Pier. Holy shit.

Jarred found a parking place not too far ahead. He was just be-yond McCormick Place. We were a bit behind schedule, and he was doing a great job of keeping everyone apprised of our progress. We couldn't pass up the waterfall on the back of Shed Aquarium. I'm pretty sure it was not supposed to be a wading pool but, my God, it felt wonderful. We immersed ourselves in that thing as if we were five-year-olds dancing in the cool waters of an open fire hydrant. We felt pretty sure the welcoming committee would understand. Truth be told, we didn't give Jarred or the welcoming committee a thought.

We caught up to Jarred, and with just a couple miles left, this was our final pit stop. We all took time to sign the back of the RV. It had become a special billboard, with signatures of many of those we had met or had run with. It also included the names of many, no longer with us, that we had run for. Ours would be the last names added. Once finished, we took photos and shared a very special moment. Then Jarred headed out. He was off to meet the welcoming party at Harry Caray's on Navy Pier. It was time for one last jaunt. Two miles to go.

We crossed under the overpass and hopped back on the trail. I'm sure it must have been forming for awhile, but appearing to show up out of nowhere was a huge thunderhead rolling into Chicago from the northwest. It didn't seem as much a storm as a giant alien craft. It was an enormous dark black cloud just big enough to cover the city. Blue sky surrounded it on all sides. Ominous.

The trails were still pretty busy, even with the heat. All types of people were out. Some were running, others biking. Some were roller skating and others just walking about. The dude, up ahead, wearing a cowboy hat, however, seemed a bit out of place. It only seemed out of place until I realized it was Eddie! He had come out to run the last mile. Aunt Patty waited with him, along with my sister Kristan and her daughter, Alyssa. It was perfect. I didn't know for sure what it meant to each of them to be there. To me, it meant everything.

The entire sky had turned black, and as the wind picked up, the rain started to fall, and the temperature did the same. It was obvious that it was going to pour, and within minutes it was doing just that.

Steven Cannon

It felt so good!! I'm sure most people were either in shelter or making a dash to find some. It was one hell of a thunderstorm. Eddy looked at us grinning. He was pretty sure this was Uncle Mike's doing. One last practical joke from above. If so, we all laughed right along with him as we continued on our way, completely drenched. The storm lasted only minutes. As we neared our final destination, the sun reappeared. The unbearable heat was gone. It was surreal.

We made the turn onto Navy Pier and were less than a half mile from the finish. Falck let every person anywhere near hear it. "This man just ran around Lake Michigan! Steve Cannon has done it!" Man, that guy has a voice. The Pier was packed. I'm pretty sure if you were within a mile of that place, you could hear Sir Falck proclaim the good news. His booming proclamations made me a bit uncomfortable at first. I quickly let go of that and allowed myself to soak in as much of the moment as possible.

I had reached the end of my forty day run around Lake Michigan. As we made the final turn towards the finish at Harry Caray's, I searched the crowd, looking for the one person who mattered at that moment. My mother was there, as always, waiting for me. Falling into her open arms, tears of joy flowed freely down our faces. I was home.

We Did It!!!

Author's Note

Thank you so much for reading Forty Days and becoming a part of my life journey. Who would have thought a kid with a score of 13 on his ACT in English could or would write a book? Thank God for great editors! I hope that something in these pages inspires you to take on your own Lake Michigan. It's okay if it scares the crap out of you. Actually that's a good thing...it means you have chosen something awesome. Keep me in the loop. I look forward to following YOUR kick-ass adventure!

Cancer sucks. The gifts of cancer do not. I have been fortunate, through my adventures, to raise money for those fighting this disease. They have taught me much about life and about the value of every moment, every relationship, and every hug. They are my heroes. I have run 292 miles across my beautiful home state of Iowa, 1,037 miles around the Great Lake Michigan, and organized a cross-country 4,000-mile relay run by and for cancer fighters. I have failed, nearly drowning during the World's longest kayak race, raced my Fat Bike in some of the coldest places on our continent and was inducted into the 2016 Order of the Hrimthurs.

The lessons and insights of all these journeys are universal in nature and can be applied to all that we do, both personally and professionally. Success and failure in each venture leaves clues. I would be honored to share these lessons and insights with your organization or personally as your coach.

Again, thank you. It blows me away that I have a book completed and a couple more in the works, but even more so that you have taken the time to read it.

Adventurously yours,

–Steve Cannon

To become a test reader for Steve's next book, hire him to speak or coach, ask a question or just say "Hi,":

- visit www.expandyourpossible.com
- Twitter/Instagram/Pinterest @runcannonrun
- "Like" 40 Days on Facebook

*"Little did I know,
my next adventure would take me
to the coldest places on Earth!"*

Coming This Winter...